BECOMING HUMAN

LIBRARY OF LIVING FAITH

JOHN M. MULDER, General Editor

BECOMING HUMAN

BY
LETTY M. RUSSELL

THE WESTMINSTER PRESS
PHILADELPHIA

BOOK DESIGN BY DOROTHY ALDEN SMITH

First edition

Published by The Westminster Press®
Philadelphia, Pennsylvania

PRINTED IN THE UNITED STATES OF AMERICA
9 8 7 6 5 4 3 2 1

Library of Congress Cataloging in Publication Data

Russell, Letty M.
  Becoming human.

  (Library of living faith)
  Bibliography: p.
  1. Man (Christian theology) 2. Salvation.
I. Title. II. Series.
BT701.2.R87   233   81-23121
ISBN 0–664–24408–4   AACR2

CONTENTS

FOREWORD

The word "theology" comes from two Greek words—
theos ("God") and *logos* ("word" or "thought"). Theology
is simply words about God or thinking about God. But for
many Christians, theology is remote, abstract, baffling,
confusing, and boring. They turn it over to the professionals—the theologians—who can ponder and inquire into
the ways of God with the world.

This series, Library of Living Faith, is for those Christians who thought theology wasn't for them. It is a collection of ten books on crucial doctrines or issues in the Christian faith today. Each book attempts to show why our
theology—our thoughts about God—matters in what we
do and say as Christians. The series is an invitation to
readers to become theologians themselves—to reflect on
the Bible and on the history of the church and to find their
own ways of understanding the grace of God in Jesus
Christ.

The Library of Living Faith is in the tradition of another
series published by Westminster Press in the 1950s, the
Layman's Theological Library. This new collection of
volumes tries to serve the church in the challenges of the
closing decades of this century.

The ten books are based on the affirmation of the Letter
to the Ephesians (4:4–6): "There is one body and one Spirit,

just as you were called to the one hope that belongs to your call, one Lord, one faith, one baptism, one God and Father of us all, who is above all and through all and in all." Each book addresses a particular theme as part of the Christian faith as a whole; each book speaks to the church as a whole. Theology is too important to be left only to the theologians; it is the work and witness of the entire people of God.

But, as Ephesians says, "grace was given to each of us according to the measure of Christ's gift" (Eph. 4:7), and the Library of Living Faith tries to demonstrate the diversity of theology in the church today. Differences, of course, are not unique to American Christianity. One only needs to look at the New Testament and the early church to see how "the measure of Christ's gift" produced disagreement and conflict as well as a rich variety of understandings of Christian faith and discipleship. In the midst of the unity of the faith, there has never been uniformity. The authors in this series have their own points of view, and readers may argue along the way with the authors' interpretations. But each book presents varying points of view and shows what difference it makes to take a particular theological position. Sparks may fly, but the result, we hope, will be a renewed vision of what it means to be a Christian exhibiting in the world today a living faith.

These books are also intended to be a library—a set of books that should be read together. Of course, not everything is included. As the Gospel of John puts it, "There are also many other things which Jesus did; were every one of them to be written I suppose that the world itself could not contain the books that would be written" (John 21:25). Readers should not be content to read just the volume on Jesus Christ or on God or on the Holy Spirit and leave out those on the church or on the Christian life or on Christianity's relationship with other faiths. For we are called to one faith with many parts.

The volumes are also designed to be read by groups of

people. Writing may be a lonely task, but the literature of the church was never intended for individuals alone. It is for the entire body of Christ. Through discussion and even debate, the outlines of a living faith can emerge.

Letty M. Russell is a United Presbyterian minister, and she teaches theology at Yale Divinity School. She is known widely for her previous work: *Human Liberation in a Feminist Perspective* (1974), *The Future of Partnership* (1979), and *Growth in Partnership* (1981). Concerning this book, she says: "My ministry has always been involved with the struggle to become human. In East Harlem we struggled against the dehumanization caused by poverty, racism, and urban neglect. As a woman I have struggled against the dehumanization that comes from sexual stereotypes and sexism. As a Christian and theologian, I come to know God through learning how to live as the human being God intends. And in knowing God I gain the insight and strength to become more human. My particular contribution in this small volume is the story and perspective of a woman on a crucial theological question: 'What does it mean to become human according to God's intention?' This contribution may broaden the perspective of those who understand human nature in a more narrowly male image."

Throughout the text, when an author's name or book is mentioned or page numbers are cited the full reference is listed under Books for Further Reading. Also included in the bibliography are books that provide general reading on the entire topic.

Readers are encouraged to read and discuss the Scripture text suggested for each chapter. Unless otherwise indicated, all Bible quotations are from the Revised Standard Version. Brackets indicate that I have substituted a word or phrase.

Names that are in parentheses in the text indicate the author or popularizer of a particular phrase or point of view.

JOHN M. MULDER

Louisville Presbyterian Theological Seminary
Louisville, Kentucky

1
SEARCHING FOR HUMANITY
Mark 5:1–20

"In kindergarten my nickname was 'Letty Spaghetti.' I was so thin (can you believe it?) that my parents put me on a diet of bananas!" As I sat with a group of church professionals, that was my contribution to the usual "get acquainted" ritual. The ritual was slightly different because we had been asked to tell not only our names but also our nicknames. One person was "Chris" for Christopher Robin. Another had no nickname because her real name, Palmera, had been invented by her parents when she was born on Palm Sunday. Still others had names given to them by sisters and brothers who couldn't pronounce the real name, or by friends in a teasing mood, or by themselves in the search for a new look. The names came out of different languages and cultures, and some of them came out of specific attempts at name-calling or ridicule.

The group could have shared family names, job descriptions, church affiliation, country of origin, or many other aspects of their individual and collective stories. In each case we would learn something about the other persons, but we would not necessarily learn their full identity. For our identity as human beings is always a problem. Each of us is so many different persons that we are never fully known to others or to ourselves. The search for our hu-

manity, both individually and collectively, is a constant
retelling and sifting out of who we are as we try to identify
the integrating meaning and purpose of our lives. One
way of searching for our humanity is to listen to the way
God addresses us and calls us by name, for it is an affirmation of the Christian faith that we are known by a God who
is *for us, not against us* (Rom. 8:31). To understand more
clearly the way that God's address is a clue in the search
for humanity let us turn to look at the story of Jesus and
the man called Legion.

My Name Is Legion

Our story in Mark 5:1–20 takes us to the far side of the
Sea of Galilee, perhaps to Gerasa, one of the Greco-Roman
towns of the Decapolis. Here Jesus encounters Everybody,
a man so full of different personalities that he is called
"Legion" (six thousand people!). In all his wild misery the
man is a "riot of persons." It is not hard to identify with
such an outcast as we experience the turmoil of the wild,
mad world of today. Often we also feel torn apart, full of
fear, and confused as we search for a way to be our true
selves, yet never seem to know what that true self looks
like.

The story of how the "riot of persons" is restored to his
right mind contains features that may have been drawn
from a Jewish folk tale. The "riot of pigs" is a dramatic sign
of the healing power of Jesus and the finality of the cure,
although originally the swine may have been a source of
amusement to Jewish hearers, who considered them un-
clean and would have been happy to hear that they
drowned. The story is told as a four-part drama.

Called by Name. Verses 1–10 describe the predicament
of the man in vivid detail. He is an outcast from society;
his home is in the tombs, among the dead. As soon as he

sees Jesus in the distance he runs and throws himself before him, shouting in a loud voice, "What is *this thing*
between you and me, Jesus?" Jesus responds by asking the
man's name. Knowing a person's name or identity is understood in biblical accounts as a way of gaining power
over that person. For instance, when God calls Moses to be
the leader of Israel, Moses not only wants a sign of miracu-
lous power but he also wants to know the name of the God
who has called him (Ex. 3:1–15).

The man's nickname, Legion, seems to indicate that he
has been declared a nonperson by his community and
condemned to living death. This experience is not uncom-
mon in our own time as communities deal with those who
are elderly, handicapped, sick, or just different by rejection, isolation, and institutionalization. Such people often
lose a sense of who they are when they are cut off from
human community. In vs. 11–13 the cure of the man,
already initiated by Jesus, is completed and the swine are
filled with the legion of demons.

Sent to Proclaim. We then notice the reaction of the
Gentile owners of the pigs. In vs. 14–17 the people in the
town are both amazed and angry over the loss of so much
property because of one "worthless" person. They find the
man no longer a "riot" but properly clothed and perfectly
sane. Jesus, the one who has brought healing, is considered
a public danger and is asked to leave. Of course, the man
wants to go with Jesus. But in vs. 18–20 we hear that Jesus
has other plans for their new story together. The man is
restored to his own community, and there, among those
who had declared him "dead," he is sent to proclaim the
good news of what God had done for him. With this new
task, Everybody becomes Somebody! He goes through the
"ten town area" to show and tell how Jesus has become the
beginning of his new history and the source of his new
identity.

HUMAN EXPERIMENT

One day recently I told a local pastor that I was eager to write a small book about what it means to be human, because this is a question that interests everyone, including me! Her response was less than enthusiastic. "I haven't noticed that anyone is going around asking what it means to be human in our parish." I realized from this small "reality check" that I was generating answers for a question that wasn't necessarily being asked by the Women's Fellowship, the Board of Trustees, or even the Youth Group. Yet questions are asked. Questions arise about who we are, what we want to become, and what we stand for as persons and as churches. These questions about the meaning of our life are questions about what it means to be human. And they are questions that are not easily answered, because being human is a problem.

Humanity as a Problem. It is as if our lives are a continuing experiment, a constant trying out of a "legion" of roles, views, moods, and thoughts to find out who we are, and who we will become. It appears to be the peculiar gift of human beings that they have the freedom to stand outside themselves and to watch what is going on around them and within them. As Jürgen Moltmann puts it, each of us is at the same time the questioner and the one questioned, and therefore each answer we find is inadequate and leads to further questions.

In the face of this freedom and openness we often draw back, retreating from the painful search through various forms of escape, such as drugs, overwork, or television addiction. At other times our retreat takes the form of accepting conclusive answers from social or religious authorities who assign our nature to us. We find it easier to "believe" that all will be well if we consume the right products and act the parts we see on television. Or we hope that all our problems will be solved by the simplistic answers and rules proclaimed by many of the popular television preachers. But there is no safe shortcut to becoming human. We have to find our own provisional answers along the way as, through our decisions, we interact with our environment, and come to name ourselves and our world, taking responsibility for our lives.

In this sense, human nature is an unfinished experiment. In the midst of our social destiny and of all the constraints of our particular life history and context, we nevertheless are faced with decisions that are made by default if we refuse to respond. The answers to the questions of our lives are not always given, but the questions themselves are important. In the words of the poet Rainer Maria Rilke, the point is to live the questions.

> Live in the questions now. Perhaps you will gradually, without noticing it, live along some distant day into the answer. (P. 35)

We try to understand our human nature by comparison with the world around us. In comparison to other living creatures, we notice that human beings are not just born. They have a long maturation process in which, through interaction with one another and with their environment, they learn how to look at the world, how to name it through language, and how to create an environment in which they can survive. In comparison with other persons and cultures, we discover that there is no one way of being human, but that the meaning of human life and action is developed in family, tribe, and nation and in the sharing of a particular culture. Often human groups and cultures define themselves over against others by declaring that their own way of life is the only human way, treating others as barbarians or nonhumans.

In the search for answers to the meaning of life, human beings look beyond themselves and the world in which they live, comparing themselves to transcendent beings. Questioning themselves, they conclude: "That's *not* all there is." They look beyond themselves toward that which will give strength and meaning in the midst of fear and confusion. For Christians, the source of that meaning is God, who shares life with us in the person of Jesus Christ. This is a God who both questions us and answers us by calling us to act in responsible stewardship of the life that has been given us as a gift.

The biblical understanding of human beings as those called by God into covenant partnership and service is only one of many ways of interpreting the source of human identity. As Perry LeFevre points out, the wide variety of interpretation is due to the fact that different philosophers and theologians emphasize different aspects of human experience (pp. 154–166). For instance, some philosophers, such as Julian Huxley, have focused on biology and the evolution of human life and culture. Others, like Karl Marx, concerned about the inhuman conditions of modern industrial life, have focused on the economic factors of production as these affect the social and personal structures on human life. Still others, like Sigmund Freud, focus on the psychological development of the individual. Theological writers also select a particular angle of vision for their descriptions of humanity. Sometimes they also begin with biology, economics, sociology, psychology, or philosophy and relate these to the biblical message. At other times they focus on particular human attributes, such as thinking, deciding, creating, communicating, or relating to others. This variety of interpretation enriches our understanding of human nature, but it leaves us with the essentially human task of searching for the meaning of our own human identity.

Human Vulnerability. If as human beings we don't really know who we are, this makes us terribly vulnerable.

We are afraid to find out who we are. In a sort of mixture of self-love and self-hate we are curious about ourselves, yet afraid that we might not really like ourselves if we know too much. We are also vulnerable to the way others decide who we are and how we should act, and often deny our own particular gifts in order to find favor with family, friends, neighbors, and employers. Others in turn are vulnerable to us if we seek to conceal our own fear by adopting a role of superiority and domination toward them. Whether or not we seek to escape ourselves through manifestations of weakness or of power, we still do not escape the fact that our human life is not a given, but must be created as we go along.

The recognition that in some sense we are our personal and social history leads us to recite the story or history of the events of our lives and world over and over in order to find clues for our present and future journey. Every time that events, actions, or interactions change our angle of vision the story must yield new clues as we search for the history that is usable in shaping our still-evolving story. This is why we rewrite history over and over again. It is why the "old, old story" of the Bible suddenly becomes a "new, new story" when God's Word is addressed to us in new circumstances.

Sometimes we, like the man called Legion, discover a new story that illuminates the meaning and purpose of our history. The demoniac was the same man after he met Jesus, but everything was different because of his new history. He lived in the same Ten Town area, yet everything was different because he had a new task. In this same sense we could say that our vulnerability as human beings is not just a problem. It is also a gift of God, for it enables us to open ourselves to others and to God in such a way that we "fall in faith" and consent to share our life story with the One who comes to dwell with us.

COMMON HUMANITY

In the face of human vulnerability it is no wonder that a major question about our common humanity concerns our rights as human beings. We find that we need protection not only from nature but also, and especially, from one another!

Humanity as a Right. Some cultures have tended to reserve the right to be treated as a human being to a particular nation, race, class, or sex. Yet, since the time of the ancient Greek and Roman Stoic philosophers, it has been argued that *all* human beings are basically alike, regardless of culture or status, because of their rational ability. In a similar way the Hebrew and Christian traditions understood all of humanity as sharing a common world destiny under the hand of their Creator. From these perspectives, the modern idea of universal human rights gradually developed in Western society. Human rights based on common humanity have been incorporated into modern constitutions in all areas of the world and are a part of the Charter of the United Nations. As Moltmann points out, these constitutional provisions are not so much formulations of existing reality as concrete expressions of the hope that human beings will come to respect the basic human needs of every person (p. 10).

It is the discrepancy between acknowledged human rights to food, clothing, shelter, work, justice, peace, and dignity, and the reality of human starvation, need, exploitation, and degradation that makes humanity a double problem. By the tyranny of political and economic systems persons are deprived of their basic rights through the use of the very technology that was supposed to liberate them from the tyranny of nature. In subhuman conditions their human nature is denied. At the same time, those who participate in societies that deprive people of their rights

are becoming subhuman in their refusal of responsibility
for their neighbors and for all creation. It is not enough to
say, "Yes we all participate in individual and social sin."
For in asking about the meaning of our own life and death,
we are confronted with the life, suffering, and death of
others, all of whom belong to God's creation. Who we are
as human beings is in part dependent on how we cultivate
the rights of others around us and all around the world.

Keeping Life Human. In situations of dehumanization
through denial of human rights we can see very clearly
some of the things that are important to all of us in "keeping human life human" (Paul Lehmann). Because we all
have our own story, there is no one definition of what it
means to be human. Each culture or subculture, each ideology, each religion explains the reality of human nature
in its own way. But in the midst of human struggles for
wholeness and meaning in life it does seem possible to
discover some of the areas of human relationship that are
crucial to keeping life human.

The first ingredient in keeping human life human is the
need to be treated as *a subject, not as an object,* of the
manipulation. In a technological world where efficiency is
so highly valued, people are often treated as objects as
they are turned into mere things or instruments for conve-
nience, profit, or manipulation. Although we see the statis-
tics of poverty, war, and suffering, and view the victims
themselves on television, we do not really *see* our faceless
neighbors. When we find human persons or groups "un-
controllable" it seems far easier to blame the victims, and
declare them nonpersons, no longer fit to live in the "civi-
lized" community. So great is our ability to ignore the
humanity of persons that the U.S. Government has been
able to announce with pride that it has developed a mar-
velous new bomb that will destroy people, not property!
Legion is still with us. But so is the One who called him by
name and affirmed his right to be treated as a subject.

A second ingredient in keeping human life human is the possibility of *participation in shaping our own future.* Because we express our humanity in creating our story and giving it meaning, we lose something essential to our life when we are without hope. Our ability to go beyond ourselves toward others and toward the future provides the ability to hope against hope even in situations of extreme persecution or suffering (Rom. 4:18). When circumstances are such that we have no perception that we can share in making even a small difference in our future, an important part of human life is denied. The chains that Legion wore and broke among the tombs were more than indications of his wild, brute strength. They were also indicators that for him the future had been denied. He was without hope, living among those already dead. Stories from persons who are imprisoned or who are suffering from physical sickness seem to indicate that the ability to resist suffering is often related to the person's ability to hope and, therefore, to continue the struggle toward change.

A third ingredient is very much related to the other two ingredients. Human beings need a *community of support* that provides a sense of being subject as well as opportunities to participate with others in shaping the future. It is from others that we learn who we are and how to name the world in which we live. And, just as important, it is from the love and care of others that we grow and live as human beings. Perhaps the most difficult aspect of Legion's life was that he was isolated from human community, left among the tombs. The pain of such experience is known to many of us as our own problems, sicknesses, or circumstances cause us to be isolated from the love and care we need so badly. Often the isolation is doubled because those who could provide community withdraw from us in fear or guilt. For instance, cancer patients testify that one of the greatest causes of their isolation is the fear, grief, and rejection of those who are well. No matter what our circumstances, we are like Legion in needing to have others with whom to share our story.

If the needs to be treated as subject, to participate in shaping our destiny, and to be supported by others are in any sense important to keeping human life human, then these needs are important human rights along with such things as food, housing, work, and health. Whatever other clues we may find in Mark's story of the Gerasene demoniac, we can certainly see in it the story of someone whose humanity was restored by the One who called him by name and sent him to proclaim the story of God's goodness among his own people.

Our search for humanity is a lifelong process of *becoming human*. Our lives are an experiment of faith in which we seek to become what God intends for us. As we reflect on our own calling in Christ, we may be helped by the discussion of four basic questions in this book. Chapters 1 and 2 ask why human nature is a problem and suggest that we look for the meaning of our humanity among the "losers" of society. Chapters 3 and 4 raise the question of who we are in relation to God's intention and interpret our destiny in the light of God's partnership with us in Jesus Christ. Chapters 5 and 6 discuss who we are as woman and man created by God, suggesting that we are both "helpers" who refuse to be radically helped. Finally, Chapters 7 and 8 ask how we can share together in becoming human and offer an invitation to join in God's freedom movement.

2
NOT QUITE HUMAN
John 4:1–42

In 1947, British author Dorothy Sayers published a book entitled *Unpopular Opinions.* In one of the essays of that book, entitled "The Human-Not-Quite-Human," she points out that there is a prevailing myth in our society that "women are unlike men." Rather than being called "the neighboring sex," they are called "the opposite sex."

> But the fundamental thing is that women are more like men than anything else in the world. They are human beings. *Vir* is male and *Femina* is female: but *Homo* is male and female. (P. 37)

Yet in the language and perception of our society this likeness is ignored since man is always understood as both human and male, and woman is only female.

This not-quite-human world that woman inhabits is a great challenge to any discussion of what it means to be human. If human is seen as male and described by men, what happens is that no one ever does find out what the human story is all about. The mechanism by which such a conspiracy of silence comes about has to do with our fear of the process of becoming human. In Chapter 1 we saw that human life is an experiment in which we must construct our own story out of our choices and the constraints of our particular context. One way of avoiding this continuing responsibility is to cut off the process, to conclude the experiment as much as possible by deciding that we have "arrived." By means of a particular set of social, political, or religious ideas we assign persons a static place and relate to them in their assigned role.

This response to our own vulnerability becomes destructive for others. In order to protect ourselves we secure our place in the social and natural order by viewing ourselves as the model of superiority. Even when it is very difficult to feel superior we can be part of a "superior group" and look down on those who are not in the group. So it happens that persons and groups that are anxious about whether they will *measure up* to the cultural standards of superiority usually *cut others down* to their size. There are many ways to cut persons down to size in a society and some of these are clearly portrayed in John's story of Jesus and the Samaritan woman.

TALKING WITH A WOMAN

It is no wonder the disciples were shocked that Jesus was talking with a woman. The story in John 4:1–42 reflects Jewish customs which viewed women as not quite human. It was considered undesirable to speak with a woman even in one's home, let alone in public. John makes good use of this dramatic incident as he draws from traditional materials to shape the two scenes of the story of a Samaritan woman called as an evangelist. Again, as in Mark 5, we find Jesus encountering a marginal person in a marginal setting outside Judea. Here too is expressed something of God's intention to offer the living knowledge of God's love in Jesus Christ to all people. John uses the story as a setting for teaching about the living water of Jesus' teaching and the universal Spirit communicated by Jesus.

Three Strikes Against Her. In vs. 1–6 John sets the scene for Jesus' conversation with the woman at the well of Jacob in Samaria. The first scene between Jesus and the woman then unfolds in vs. 7–26. In the midst of the discussion and the misunderstanding of his request for a drink of water, the woman slowly comes to faith that the one with whom she speaks is the Messiah. The whole conversation seems very improbable, because the woman has three strikes against her. She is foreign, fallen, and female! But this does not seem to matter when the Word needs to get out. At the tomb it was the women who were to be the first witnesses to the resurrection (Luke 24:1–11), and here at the well it is a woman who first carries the message that Jesus is the Messiah.

The pattern of maintaining one's special human identity over against other groups is certainly seen in the relationship of the Jews of Jesus' time to those of "mixed blood" who lived in Samaria and worshiped God on Mt. Gerizim rather than at the Temple in Jerusalem. The woman is surprised that Jesus would even consider drinking out of her water pot, let alone speak to her, because Samaritans were considered by the Jews to be ritually impure and were not to be associated with. One Jewish regulation from A.D. 65–66 warns that one can never count on the ritual purity of Samaritan women, since they are menstruants from the cradle (Lev. 15:19; Raymond E. Brown).

She was not only a foreigner, like the "good" Samaritan of Luke 10:30–37. The woman was also a sinner, at least by standards of Jewish custom. Jews were allowed three marriages and she had had five and was now living with a sixth man. The detail of her story seems to have been included to reveal that Jesus was a prophet in knowing and sharing her life story (vs. 16–19).

The second scene, in vs. 27–38, moves the woman into the background as she runs to share her new faith by telling the men of the town about the Messiah. This enables John to present the discussion of Jesus and the disciples about his mission, which is being fulfilled in the response of the Samaritans to his message. But the opening of the scene, as well as the conclusion of the story in vs. 39–42, indicates that the greatest offense of Jesus' partner at the well was simply that she was *a woman.* Not only did she offend the disciples, she also found herself discounted by her own countrymen, who made it clear that their faith was finally not dependent on her story but on hearing for themselves that Jesus is the Savior of the world. Like the women at the tomb, the woman at the well is called to witness among those who consider her words "an idle tale" (Luke 24:11).

For Her, Not Against Her. Often in our reading of this story we focus on the meaning of living water and of true worship and fail to notice the meaning of Jesus' actions. As in many of the Gospel accounts, Jesus is portrayed relating to the woman, beyond the stereotypes of custom, as a fully human being. Far from considering her discussion with him "a bunch of idle gossip," Jesus carries on a very interesting theological conversation in which the Samaritan woman, like Martha (John 11:1–27; Luke 10:38–42), comes to acknowledge and share the truth of which he speaks. As Rachel Conrad Wahlberg has pointed out, Jesus seems to like "uppity women" who respond to him, discussing theological points about which they are supposed to know nothing (pp. 9, 89–103). Dorothy Sayers reminds us:

> It was no wonder that women were first at the Cradle and last at the Cross. They had never seen a man like this Man. . . . Nobody could possibly guess from the words and deeds of Jesus that there was anything "funny" about women's nature. (P. 47)

The Samaritan woman has many scars from a long history of marriages, yet this does not prevent Jesus from calling her to a new history as one who has a task among her community and therefore a new future to which she is called as a participant. Jesus' presence among her com-

munity makes it possible for her to be restored to a community of faith where the living water of his Spirit can
transcend all the ways persons are cut down to not-quite-
human size. Thus in John's account the message that God
had sent Christ so that the world might be saved was heard
and believed among the peasants of Samaria even though
it was rejected by the teachers of Jerusalem (John 3; Raymond E. Brown).

CREATION AND CREATURES

Why could peasants hear and believe what learned
teachers could not? Perhaps in part because as human
beings we tend to see and hear what we have been taught
to see and hear. Our point of view is shaped by our particular context and history. Those in a position of privilege
certainly can hear God's Word when it is addressed to
them in the power of the Spirit. Yet they have less incen-
tive to change their view of "the way things are supposed
to be" than those who have nothing to lose from such a
change.

Myths of Origin. One way of establishing "the way
things are supposed to be" is by putting these social, religious, and political customs under the authority of the
past. Through describing "the way things have always
been" we convince one another that this is the way we
must live and act as human beings. Myths of origin are
always important to us as we search out clues for our journey of life. But often those myths of origin, like Genesis 1
to 3, that are so very rich in meaning are also rich in
misunderstanding. Thus it is no accident that the cultural
tradition that has sprung, in part, out of the Greek and
Hebrew heritage views both women and nature as something to be dominated and subdued. The description of
human sin in Genesis 3 is misused to establish the fact that
husbands "shall rule over" wives and that "the ground is

cursed" (vs. 16, 17). In this view of creation and creature, woman and all the natural world have been degraded. Male is seen as human and everything else as not quite human.

If this seems farfetched, we have only to think about the description of the "search for humanity" in Chapter 1. The discussion compared human beings to other living creatures and parts of creation, to people of other cultures, and to that which transcends humanity. In such a comparison the usual assumption is that human beings, because of their intellectual and spiritual capacity, are *better* than the rest of the animate and inanimate world, and somehow akin to that which transcends the creaturely part of human life. If we assume that our intellectual life makes us most human, the implication seems to be that our bodily life and needs make us most like the animals. In the Christian tradition women have frequently been associated with this bodily, natural part that is to be transcended. Following the pattern of "more or less spiritual," the tendency is to see levels of life in a hierarchy with God and men at the top and women and animals at the bottom. The consequences of this view of reality are that nature and women become objects of exploitation. This is justified by an appeal to "Father rights" over against the "human rights" and "nature rights" that are violated (Marie Augusta Neal).

There have been a variety of ways for searching out what interdependence between human beings and nature might look like. In an article in the book *The Human and the Holy*, Chung Choon Kim of Korea suggests that we usually look at the relationship of humanity to nature in one of three ways (pp. 98–108). We speak of ourselves as creatures who are biologically a part *of nature*, and study ourselves from the point of view of biology or even sociobiology. At the same time we function as workers who are related *to nature* through the use of tools and technology.

Through science we study ways of doing things to our
environment. Lastly we may see ourselves as stewards
who are responsible *for nature* and opposed to its exploitation and destruction. Through the study of ecology we try
to find ways in which nature can be protected from humanity.

Perhaps one way to balance these three views is to see
ourselves as partners *with nature* who recognize the
mutuality of our life with all creatures and creation. We
are all part of nature and nature is part of us. It shares in
our common destiny and history, just as we share in the
rhythms of the interconnected chain of life. This sharing
of human destiny has led all of nature to "groan in travail,"
according to Paul, as it waits for the coming of God's New
Creation in which creatures and creation will become
partners (Rom. 8:18–23).

A New Point of View. How can we move beyond a
purely instrumental view of the world around us which
allows us to "manhandle the earth" and whatever else is
viewed as not quite human (James Parks Morton)? One
way is to allow our view of reality to be changed, or to let
ourselves "be transformed by the renewal of [our]
mind[s]" (Rom. 12:2). *The Predicament of the Prosperous*
reminds us that such a change of perception is difficult,
especially when it calls for sacrifice or change of life-style
on our part (pp. 57–75). The perception of the world
around us that dominates the thinking of Western society
today is a hierarchical point of view that is not good for the
health of either creatures or creation, ourselves included.
We tend to order things in an ascending order of value and
authority in order to structure human relationships in a
clear pattern that keeps everyone and everything in an
assigned place.

Often it is this way of seeing things and of structuring
our relationships which squeezes out the possibility of in-
novation and change, and discourages the possibility of

developing common bonds of community with one another and with nature. Such a model of the way things are
is seen not just in the military, the government, or business. It is seen also in church structures which have bish-
ops and ministers at the top and women and children at
the bottom. These same churches frequently preach about
community and partnership, but do not encourage alternative ways of relating that promote interdependence.

If we follow the attitude of Jesus in being "for, not
against" those who are on the underside of the *pyramid
of domination,* we must seek to see and understand our
world in a perspective of cooperation and partnership.
When, consciously or unconsciously, reality is seen in the
form of a pyramid or hierarchy, everything is judged in
terms of super- or sub-ordination. Things tend to be assigned a "divine order," with God at the top, men next,
and so on down the ladder to dogs, plants, and "imper-
sonal" nature. In this scheme of the world, unity is
achieved by subduing everything to the group on top.
Those people, ideas, or things that do not fit because they
are foreign, weak, or disruptive are pressed down or out
of the picture so that they disappear from consideration.
In this view of reality, to be truly human is to achieve
power and superiority within the pyramid of domination.
Those who don't make it because of sex, age, class, race,
or nationality are simply not quite human.

Yet it is possible to see reality as a *rainbow of partnership.* The world around us perceived in this way resem-
bles a wide spectrum of colors, people, and ideas, all of
which might contribute to the possibility of cooperation
and partnership in the midst of diversity. In this perception of things, unity is achieved through respecting the
diversity of creation and creatures, and seeking to include
them in a synergetic model of partnership where the
whole is greater than the sum of the parts. People who
might not "fit" expand the dimensions of the spectrum. In

this rainbow perspective our understanding of what it means to be human is continually multiplied and extended to include partnership with the not quite human and with nature as well.

It is difficult to look at the world from a new point of view and to change many of our most "sacred" views of things. Yet this is just what we are called to do through our commitment to Jesus Christ. As Paul reminds us in II Cor. 5:16–21, we are no longer to regard anyone from a human point of view, but rather from the point of view of Christ's death and resurrection. All persons and all creation are to be viewed as objects of God's love for whom Christ died and was raised. Through baptism into Christ we belong to a new order of things in which we no longer look for human authority in hierarchy, but for the basis of all authority in the actions of God who has overcome all divisions and has reunited us (Isa. 43:18–21; Gal. 6:14–15).

> When anyone is united in Christ, there is a new world; the old order has gone, and a new order has begun. (II Cor. 5:17, NEB)

God's Reversals

New Creation has begun to take form in our lives through the life, death, and resurrection of Jesus Christ, and it is sometimes visible along our journey through small signs of the Spirit breaking into our lives. We catch glimpses of this new reality in the biblical stories of the way God is at work among us to establish God's will "on earth as it is in heaven" (Matt. 6:10). One thing we notice as we share these stories of God's kingdom is that God's view of reality is different from what we might expect. There are many unexpected reversals in the stories: talents that are used multiply; people who work only the last hour receive a day's wage; those saved are lost; the poor are fed and the rich sent empty away.

God's Arithmetic. This same strange arithmetic of God seems to be at work in the story of the Samaritan woman in which the least likely person becomes the bearer of good news (Hans-Ruedi Weber). Over and over the biblical stories witness to a God who has set about mending creation by means of rather unexpected persons and events. Who would guess that a marginal group of Hebrews would be the bearers of the news that God is the creator and liberator of all humankind? God chooses concrete historical contexts in which to bring about healing and restoration of wholeness, and these contexts are often the very situations of bondage, suffering, and defeat which have so dehumanized life in the Old Creation.

In God's way of viewing reality it would seem that things don't add up "right." Defying the human "logic of equivalence," the logic of Jesus and of God is one of excess, generosity, and superabundance, the logic of grace (Paul Ricoeur). It is also a logic that often bids us turn the other cheek or go the second mile, and thus stands in opposition to our "natural tendencies" (Matt. 5:38–42). This is underlined by Jesus' parables of the kingdom which, over and over, *dis*orient us in order to *re*orient us toward God's reality. While myths *establish* the existing world by putting things under the authority of the past, the parables *subvert* the world into becoming what God intends it to be. As John Dominic Crossan puts it, parables show us "the seams and edges of myth" (pp. 56–60). They make us aware of the relativity of all our self-presumptions and the absurdity of our most firm convictions.

Jesus' own actions were parabolic because they challenged the status quo and present us with a different view of what it takes to keep human life human. Neither his actions nor his words present us with just one coherent world view, be it that of the pyramid of domination or the rainbow of partnership or some other perception of the way the world should function. Rather, they tell us about the reality of God's kingdom and question the way we all look at reality. They ask how those who structure things in hierarchy include all those marginal people and groups into God's kingdom of mercy. They also ask those who want to include all people in community how they will speak the word of judgment on injustice which is part of God's kingdom of righteousness. In learning to expect the unexpected of God's reversals we perhaps can learn a little humility about ourselves in discovering that in many ways it is ourselves who turn out to be not quite human.

Superstars and Losers. In the light of the unexpected nature of God's reversals it would not be surprising if in our search for humanity we were to find an important clue in a rather unexpected place. Human identity is always a mystery that eludes us as we question ourselves and others. Since we are uneasy about living with the questions, our usual way of understanding who we are is to seek "role models," people we admire who seem to embody the qualities that seem most meaningful for our lives. Usually those models are *superstars* who have excelled in wisdom, strength, beauty, power, or goodness. Much of our examination and rewriting of history, and of our personal storytelling, involves this search for superstar persons and groups whose story seems to lend credibility and direction to our own existence. Depending on a particular need, for instance, George Washington is remembered as father of our country, honest man, elite slave owner, knowledgeable surveyor of land, winning general, husband of Martha, or namesake of a bridge.

Role models are crucial to the human experiment of finding out who we are whether the role models are found in history, literature, on the television, or among our family, friends, and acquaintances. But one of the difficulties of this process is that our favorite role models are superstars. They are *not* like us. They embody some of the things we think we would like to become. Perhaps, if we take the idea of God's arithmetic seriously, we would be well advised to look for a clue to the meaning of humanity among the *losers* of society. This is, of course, the point of looking at two such similar stories about Jesus and the losers in Mark 5 and John 4. Somehow it is the losers who seem to get the message of God's love and who seem to be able to communicate that message of meaning and hope to other people.

Why is it that the losers might help us to see our humanity more clearly? First, because we all have a great deal in common with these people and we are more likely to be nurtured in our God-given humanity if we share in their story rather than cultivate a "superstar inferiority complex." Secondly, and more important, because God has chosen to reveal Godself among just such people. Jesus was not only a male, a Jew, and a nobody, he was also a failure by ordinary standards. The cross is a place for losers, not for superstars.

> God chose what is low and despised in the world, even things that are not, to bring to nothing things that are, so that no human being might boast in the presence of God. (I Cor. 1:28)

It is the not-quite-human person who lives under circumstances that reveal the brokenness of God's creation. The "loser status" itself is not to be valued or emulated. We are not urged to live among the tombs in chains or to have 5 plus husbands. What is important to our understanding of our humanity is the losers' ability to respond to the offer of judgment and mercy and to know what it means to be given new life and room to breathe. Their story, their struggle, and their discovery of the gift of new life in the midst of living death can become a sign for us of God's intention for justice and freedom. We in turn become more human as we identify with God's invitation and the needs of the "least of these" sisters and brothers.

God has welcomed the not quite human, whoever that might be, into the heart of God's new community. Those of us who accept this invitation join the woman of Samaria as we try to show and tell the message that to be human is to be loved—by a very "illogical" God.

Recently I attended a panel at a college class reunion that addressed itself to the question of how one copes with life in more-than-middle age. The moderator began by apologizing for the panel (a familiar pattern among women). There were not going to be any outstanding speakers because it would seem that the best advice on life would come from ordinary people "like ourselves" rather than those with brilliant careers who make us look like losers. The not so unexpected happened. "Ordinary women" who were coping with terminal cancer, early widowhood, unemployability, aging parents, and wandering children didn't appear to be ordinary at all. In fact, the losers were the very ones who helped us understand our human journey a little bit better. The search for humanity may often lead us to look to those considered not quite human to show us the way toward God's intended future.

3
HUMAN DESTINY
Psalm 8

I was deep in discussion with a group of seminary students about God's purpose for our lives. In the middle of our struggle to understand what the author of Psalm 8 was trying to say about life's destiny, I suddenly blurted out, "You know, the Westminster Shorter Catechism says that the chief end of man, and woman, is to glorify God and enjoy God forever." I had not thought of that particular Reformed formulation for years, but there it was in front of us. At ten years of age I had memorized the questions and answers of the Catechism when joining the church and now I had used a piece of my personal history as a clue to interpreting the psalmist's assertion that God has crowned us "with glory and honor" (Ps. 8:5).

No sooner had I shared this piece of church tradition with the group than one of the more outspoken women asked what, probably, they were all thinking. "Do you really believe that?" I gave the usual "scholar's answer," that it depends on what we mean by the phrase. Then I had to go home and study John Calvin's Catechism in order to figure out what I did mean. Was this still an important clue to God's intention for humanity? In this case, I decided that it could be a clue if we follow Karl Barth's view that in the New Testament "to glorify" means to make oneself or someone else appear as the

person truly is (*The Faith of the Church*, p. 26). Certainly
I would be most happy if I could glorify God by living the
way God truly intends me to live, and thus allowing God's
image to shine forth in my human existence. The idea that
human beings are created to reveal what God truly is may
seem difficult to understand, and even more difficult to
live out. Nevertheless, the Catechism question and answer
does provide us with a clue in our search for humanity. It
points to a possible destiny for our lives and leads us to ask
with the psalmist, "What are human beings that God is
mindful of them?"

A LITTLE LESS THAN GOD

When we first read Psalm 8 it seems to be giving glory
to *man*, not to God. In our own self-preoccupation we
tend to skip over the first three verses and notice only the
repetition of the Genesis 1 account of the creation of
human beings in God's image. But when we listen to what
the psalmist is saying, we hear the entire psalm as a doxology or song of praise to God. From the first word to the
last, it is not the creature or the creation but the Creator
who receives honor.

Glory to God. Perhaps in looking at the broad expanse
of the heavens, the psalmist is reminded of the God who
is creator of heaven and earth (v. 3; Artur Weiser). Everyone, even children, are bound to praise a God who has
brought the world out of darkness and chaos (Ps. 8:2; Gen.
1:1–2). In v. 4 the psalmist reflects on the relationship of
human beings to their maker. In spite of human insignifi-
cance, God has been gracious in honoring them. Verses
5–8 contain the only reference to the idea that humanity
reflects the image of God besides that in Gen. 1:26–28
(Gerhard von Rad). This idea is linked with the task or
commission given to human beings to represent God in
"mastery" of God's earth and all its creatures.

As we shall see in the chapter on human nature, the image of God seems to reflect an ancient Near Eastern metaphor for royalty, who are understood as icons or images of god, given divine commission to rule (Phyllis Bird). In the biblical material, however, the metaphor has shifted, so that the entire community becomes the representation of God and not just the king. The thought pattern of this psalm raises considerable difficulty for feminists because of the traditional translation and interpretation of v. 4 as, "What is man . . . ?" and for ecologists because of the interpretation of v. 6 that dominion means domination. The pattern of kingship tends to reinforce the power of male ruling figures rather than the power of a gracious God who stoops to care for mortals and bids them share in that caring.

The editors working on the revision of the RSV Old Testament aid our concerns for inclusiveness by correctly translating the word 'adam as "human being" in v. 4, but remind us that the psalmist and the Hebrew culture still thought of man as the model of human by leaving the male pronoun "him": "What is a human being that you are mindful of him . . . ?" Ecologists and exegetes remind us that the idea of dominion is one of responsible stewardship, but the power of the hierarchical myth is difficult to break when human beings use technology to become a "little *more* than God."

Perhaps we would be less quick to move toward such pretension if we remembered that human glory is a reflection of God's glory and honor. The prayer of our Lord is that God's name be hallowed or honored, *not* our own (Matt. 6:9). This honoring takes the form of allowing God to be seen through our lives, letting God be truly known as God chooses to be known. From the Christian perspective, there is only one person who is able to represent God in the fullness of humanity, and this is Jesus Christ. In Jesus, God glorifies us by showing us just how mindful God is of our need for forgiveness and new humanity. At the same time God glorifies Godself through gracious favor shown to us all.

God's Favor. It would seem that one of the best clues to the interpretation of Psalm 8 in Christian perspective is found in the echoes of the angels' chorus in Luke 2:14: "Glory to God in the highest, and on earth peace, good will toward [people]" (KJV). Here the angels proclaim that God is glorified and honored by God's own gracious favor or goodwill in sending Jesus Christ to all humanity. Their words are not just a hymn of praise, they are a description of what has already begun to happen in the birth of a Savior (I. Howard Marshall). God exercises dominion in being gracious to us all, for God is a *humanist,* the One who cares enough about human beings to offer them the gift of Shalom, of peace on earth.

Here we see that in God's actions, glory, dominion, and graciousness interpret each other. God's actions reveal the glory of God's true identity, and those actions of dominion are exercised in gracious restoration of peace, righteousness, and justice to the earth. God's intention for us as human beings is grace: unmerited love, favor, or mercy. To fulfill that intention in our own lives would be to share that gift of divine favor with others. To give God glory is clearly not to shout, "What is man? What is man?" in a loud voice (even from outer space). It is to become what God intends: persons who can respond in gracious love to God and to all God's creatures and creation. To exercise dominion is to share in God's gracious action of bringing peace and wholeness to the world. Lest we forget this, we have the living memory of the Prince of Shalom before us, pointing us to the reality of God's rule on earth and reminding us that our destiny is to exercise dominion in being gracious to others, even to the point of becoming "nobody" on behalf of our partners in need.

ANTICIPATING NEW CREATION

Perhaps it would seem more "logical" to look more closely at who we are as human beings before we look at what we are intended to become. But this is not the way God's logic works. In God's arithmetic things begin from the other end. They begin with God's promise of a New Creation and a New Humanity (Jer. 31:31–34; Rev. 21: 1–4). It is life according to God's activity for New Creation that is described in Jesus' parables of the kingdom or rule of God, and it is in this direction that Jesus pointed with his teaching. His own life, death, and resurrection was an anticipation of New Creation, the firstfruits of the fulfill- ment of God's promise (I Cor. 15:20–24). In the same way we are called to live each day by "thinking future while acting present" (Ted Peters, pp. 109–120).

Self-Fulfilling Prophecy. As historical beings our per- sonal and collective histories are shaped by the destiny we seek. We come to know who we are by discovering our *destiny,* and then by interpreting our present and past in the light of this *destination* (Roger Shinn). All of us have visions of the future that operate consciously or uncon- sciously as self-fulfilling prophecy. It is only as we try to correct these visions in the light of God's promised inten- tion for New Creation that we are able to anticipate God's purpose for our lives.

In a world of rapid change, not only our past history but also our future history operates as fate. We move into the future so fast that our plans for the future are usually too late before they are even formulated. For this reason futurology, or the study of the future, has been developed to forecast events and search for alternative futures from which to choose. With the use of computers and sophis- ticated analysis, scientists of the future, or futurists, are able to say what is likely to happen in the next twenty years, especially in the area of technological development. Even though the most likely thing to happen is some change that was not forecast, the descriptions of future alternatives are very important for planning. Yet they can also be dangerous if they are used as a means of gaining domination over the earth.

The groups of people who forecast the future are usually those who have the power, finances, and technology to seek control and domination over others. For instance, the most sophisticated forecasting is related to the arms race between the United States and Russia. The forecasts for the future tell who will destroy the earth first, and how many times over! Even when futurists study human needs such as distribution of food and resources, decisions to intervene and change a national or an international policy regarding land or sea rights or development funds are usually made on the basis of military and political interests of the dominant groups rather than on the basis of human or nature rights. According to Jack Nelson, the greatest proportion of development aid from the United States goes to nations considered to be our allies and not to those who are in the greatest need (p. 22).

It often happens that futurology becomes self-fulfilling prophecy. Disaster is described and the world moves toward it, even when other alternatives present themselves. Such futurology is not in itself a contradiction of the future that God intends. It becomes so only when the forecasts of the future become a tool for domination and destruction.

In order to bring about social, political, and economic change, the world needs large numbers of persons and groups with what Jürgen Moltmann calls "Utopian consciousness" (pp. 41–45). This is a consciousness that is critical of the present forms of social domination and dehumanization and is looking to a future that is more humane for all persons, more worth living. Such persons are uto-

pian not in the sense that they look to a future which can
never exist, but rather in the sense that the future can be
envisioned now as a good place in which to exist. This
vision then becomes the impulse for change in the present
through concrete actions to contradict the structures of
domination which deny people their human dignity in our
communities and across the world.

Beginning from the Other End. Envisioning or hoping
has to go along with planning and action if the "Utopian
consciousness" is to make a difference in our world. Together the vision and the concrete plans make possible an
anticipation of God's intention for humankind in the present. Together they point to the intention for the mending
of creation, and of us, by raising up signs and anticipations
of that healing and wholeness. In small actions we can
share this utopian process by such things as advocating
housing for the elderly or alternatives to incarceration;
through opposing the arms race, or supporting the poor in
their struggles to build their communities and raise their
families.

For Christians the vision of the future is understood not
as futurology but as eschatology. Eschatology is thought or
knowledge about end, purpose, or destiny. This science or
way of thinking is different from futurology because it
begins from the other end, from God's future. Futurology
asks *when* things will happen *if* they happen, and works
to direct the evolution of these events. Eschatology, on the
other hand, asks how to live now *as if* the vision of God's
purpose or goal for our lives were already present. It
presses us to make our lives "count for something" because God counts on us. People who live out their eschatology, not in waiting for the end to come, but in working to bring God's ends into the middle of personal and
social history suffer from *advent shock.* They suffer from
a maladjustment with the present because of the longed-
for future of God. This contrasts with what Alvin Toffler

has called *future shock,* maladjustment with the present
because of the longed-for past.

Jesus himself was very much maladjusted to his present.
He saw his ministry as one that was an anticipation of New
Creation. Thus in his sermon in the synagogue in
Nazareth, Jesus described his ministry in the words of
Isaiah 61, saying that he had received God's Spirit to pro-
claim good news to the poor, release to the captives, sight
for the blind, and liberty for the oppressed (Luke 4:16–30).
These were all signs of "the year of the Lord's favour" (v.
19, NEB). In the Hebrew tradition this was God's Jubilee
Year, a time of God's graciousness in which the slaves were
freed, debts forgiven, and the land restored so that crea-
tion could be mended (Lev. 25:1–34). And this is where
Jesus began, with the announcement that the time of
God's grace had arrived.

In the advent of the Coming One, the other end of
history has *already,* but *not yet,* arrived. The end has
come and is to be seen in Jesus Christ, but it is not fully
arrived. There is more to come! As part of this advent
time we can begin to live now, *as if* it were possible for
the "lame to walk and the blind to see." If we do, then it
may be that they *will.* God intends us to give glory by
anticipating the signs of God's intention in our actions
now. In this way we show what God truly is, a utopian
God!

PARTNERS IN NEW CREATION

God is a utopian God because God does not give up on
us as human beings. Contrary to the opinion of skeptics,
God is not *our* utopia or an unreal projection of our need
for salvation. We are *God's* utopia, because God has
created us and bids us become what God intends us to be.
In the face of mounting evidence of inhumanity and bro-

kenness, God is a "hopeless optimist." And because God hopes for us, we can continue to hope against hope (Rom. 8:20-21; Jürgen Moltmann).

Gracious God. In the latter part of his life, Karl Barth wrote an essay published in English under the title *The Humanity of God.* In this reflective essay he pointed out that "God is *human.*" In freely choosing to be gracious to human beings by affirming them in the humanity of Jesus Christ, God has chosen to share humanity with them as partner (p. 51). In our contemporary language we would say that God is a humanist, one who is an advocate of human beings, who cares about their destiny and shares it with them. This does not mean that God is less than God, but rather that God chooses to be with humanity and to be known in our midst.

Language about human beings and the meaning of humanity in relation to God and creation changes as the social perception of what it means to be human changes. For instance, Barth himself was famous for most of his life as a theologian who emphasized the transcendent freedom of God and the infinite separation between that God and human beings. Against those who were boastful of human honor he emphasized human sin and weakness. The Latin word for human being, *homo,* seems to reflect this low opinion of human nature, because the word is related to *humus,* earth. In the same way Genesis 2 and 3 relates the Hebrew word for humankind, *'adam,* to the word for the dust of the earth, *'adama,* of which Adam was fashioned (Gen. 2:7).

Even in the Middle Ages, according to Moltmann, humanity denoted lowliness and capacity for error in contrast to God's eternity (p. 12). In modern Western society the word "humanist" has come to mean one who advocates the importance of human beings, sometimes even by denying the importance or existence of God. Nevertheless, Christians should be humanists just because of the existence of God. They can affirm the value of every human being as the subjects of God's gracious love. In becoming human in Jesus Christ, God has shown that human beings are not to be considered lowly or of no account because God has chosen to share history and destiny with them.

Our destiny is to become *New People* as participants in New Creation. We are to be New People who are able to dwell in partnership with God, with creation, with others, and with ourselves. In the light of the other end of history, the psalmist's question, "What is a human being?" is answered by the discovery of what happens when Jesus Christ is present among us. The testimony of the early church was that the presence of Christ among two or three who are gathered together in his name brings a new focus of relationship in the common history of Jesus Christ that sets us free for others. This is what happened to the man called Legion and to the woman at the well and to countless others whose lives were transformed by the sharing of Christ's story and Christ's freedom.

This new life of participation, communion, community, or partnership is described as *koinonia* in New Testament Greek. Koinonia is a key New Testament word for sharing with someone or something and usually stresses a common bond in Jesus Christ. It is a participation in and with Christ that establishes mutual community. Paul and the early church expressed the meaning of their new humanity by pointing to the way Christ was already at work transforming their lives by the power of the Spirit. In this happening of co-humanity they discovered small anticipations of God's intended partnership in New Creation. Thus Paul describes partnership in the Lord's Supper with these words:

The cup of blessing which we bless, is it not a *koinonia* in the blood of Christ? The bread which we break, is it not a *koinonia* in the body of Christ? (I Cor. 10:16)

Gracious Neighbor. At the time of Martin Luther, the most perplexing issue for people was how to find a gracious God. Thus, in *The Bondage of the Will* Luther declares:

If I lived and worked to all eternity, my conscience would never reach comfortable certainty as to how much it must do to satisfy God.

The good news for Luther's time was that in Christ, God's gracious forgiveness was sure. In a world of fear, superstition, and death "a mighty fortress" was needed as a helper "amid the flood of mortal ills prevailing." But in our time the question that seems most unsettling to us is, "How can I find a gracious neighbor?" (Horst Symanowski). To be forgiven by our neighbor and to forgive our neighbor becomes an urgent need in the face of the divisions of race, sex, class, age, and nationality. We are often at the point of despair over whether there can even be one humanity, let alone gracious neighbors at home, on our own street, or across the world. Sometimes it seems that the best we can come up with to show our neighborliness is a "Welcome Wagon" bent on showing common consumer products. In the midst of a "lonely crowd" the affirmation that God intends us to be partners comes as welcome news!

Yet a gracious God and a gracious neighbor go together. The presence of God in Christ as our *Neighbor* in the world means that every person has become our partner (Karl Barth). To be a partner is to live according to our human destiny. This happens only in bits and pieces as we anticipate God's new reality, but when it does, we discover that this happening of co-humanity is a gift. Stewardship of that gift requires a deep *commitment* to one another and to a common goal that transcends the particular partnership and helps to hold it together. The new relationship as partner is never without *common struggle,* risk, and growth as it partakes of the ever changing and growing nature of all human relationships. Partnerships among groups or among persons depend on a willingness to share mutual responsibility and trust so that equality and inequality may be shared. In this growing interdependence there is constant interaction with the *wider community* of persons, social structures, values, and beliefs that form the context of a partnership.

When Christ is at the center of a new focus of relationship, his story becomes the common story of a Christian community engaged in common commitment and struggle in the wider community context. In such koinonia we may discover others as gracious neighbors and also learn to be gracious neighbors and partners on behalf of others. The story of the good Samaritan becomes one story, along with many biblical stories, of caring that we struggle to make our own through gracious actions of service (Luke 10:25–37). Whether we are gathered in communities of two or three, or of four or five thousand persons, the koinonia-creating presence of Christ provides us with an unexpected multiplication of gifts and energy that can give us strength to be neighbor to others along the way.

This possibility of partnership is what continues to keep our human life human as we discover that we too can be taken up into God's gracious care. In it we find clues to God's intention for our lives, and what it is to be human. For to be a human being is not just to be a man. Nor is it just to be a woman. This is why it is no more accurate to entitle books, like this one on theological anthropology, *Man* than it would be to entitle them *Woman,* for anthropology is the study of human beings. A human being is man or woman, but much more than that, a human being is God's intended partner. The discovery of God's gracious offer of partnership is the rediscovery of the chief end of man and woman. For in Christ, God accepts us as partners and lets the glory of divine partnership shine through into our lives.

4
MORE THAN HUMAN
Philippians 2:1–11

In the spring of every year a human rhythm is played out in countless graduation exercises. These ceremonies, begun in nursery school, do not end even at high school, college, or graduate school. In the form of continuing education credits and honorary degrees the ceremonies pursue us, with all their pomp and circumstance, through our funeral eulogy and sometimes beyond. Why is it that we seem to have to keep telling ourselves and one another over and over again that we *are* somebody? Perhaps because all the degrees are alike. They are *Somebody/Nobody degrees.* Not only are they used by "somebodies" to tell persons who don't have degrees that they are "nobodies," the degrees are even ambiguous for the "degree holders." The ambiguity of our unfinished histories is such that we become "somebody" through some particular accomplishment, only to discover that, after we graduate, we are "nobody" and have to start over again.

For instance, students graduating from seminary are full of pride and excitement. Now, if they can gain the added blessing of their church, they will at last become ministers! But then they begin again. "What is it to minister? What service do I perform? Why didn't they tell me that a minister is a nobody—a servant?"

This familiar sense of insecurity is part of the *S/N degree*. We spend our lives searching for who we are and keep getting a double answer. Perhaps this is more of an answer than we suspect. In the discussion of not-quite-human persons we discovered that one clue to our search for identity was that humanity is to be discovered in weakness, among those whom society considers no-account. This clue is confirmed by God's actions in Jesus Christ. In Christ, God has chosen to be with us as a *nobody* to show us what it means to be *somebody*. Paul points to this story of God's action through the One who humbled himself as a help and encouragement to all of us.

HE HUMBLED HIMSELF

The congregation at Philippi in Macedonia was the first church that Paul founded in Europe and it was visited by him on at least two occasions (Acts 16:11-40; 20:1-6). One of Paul's reasons for writing to his good friends in Philippi appears to be to set them straight concerning the facts of his imprisonment so that they will be more eager to share with him in the joyous task of serving the gospel of Christ through humility and suffering. Paul first urges them to overcome their disunity by following his own example of humility, and then turns to the example of Christ (Phil. 2:1-11).

Partners in the Gospel. In the salutation of the letter to the Philippians, Paul speaks of himself and Timothy as slaves *(douloi)* of Christ (1:1-11). Passing over his title as apostle, Paul says that he is a slave or servant of Christ to whom he has given his whole life (I Cor. 1:1). This servanthood he shares with Timothy and all those who are partners *(koinonoi)* in grace (Phil. 1:7). The Philippians share with Paul in their offering of money, in their faith, and in their willingness to share in his suffering so that the gospel

may be proclaimed. He gives thanks to God for their faith
even in the moment of his imprisonment, and looks forward to the completion of God's work among them at the
coming of the final day of Christ (vs. 3, 6).

The theme of humility, obedience, and joy is picked up
by Paul in Phil. 2:1–4 as he appeals for unity in the life of
the Christian community so that the dissent and self-pride
may not hinder the communication of the gospel. In Paul's
mind the Christian life has one purpose, to spread the
good news of God's gracious action of redemption in Jesus
Christ. Thus, for instance, Paul has assured the anxious
Philippians that he is well, in spite of everything, because
the gospel is being advanced through his imprisonment.
His humiliation and slavery in jail are of no ultimate importance because he is there as a servant of the Lord. In
contrast to the Greek understanding of humility as a sub-
servient attitude of a lower-class person, Paul speaks of
humility like that of Christ, lowly service done by a noble
person (Kenneth Crayston).

It is more likely that Paul was writing from the jail at
Ephesus than from the much greater distance of Rome,
since there seems to be rather close contact between himself and the Philippians (II Cor. 1:8–11). It is no accident
that the themes of partnership in the Spirit and joy in
suffering emerge under such circumstances (Phil. 2:1–2).
Just as modern letters from prison in Buchenwald, Bir-
mingham, Buenos Aires, and too many other places call us
to faithfulness as followers of Christ, Paul's letters from
prison bring the Spirit-filled insight of one who has found
out what it means to share the humanity of Christ. In our
time theology is being written in hymns, poems, and stories on scraps of paper and declarations of rights smuggled
out of prisons and out of police states. With Wan Sang Han
of Korea they tell us that their weakness and powerless-
ness before the "authorities" brings with it the gift of
strength to witness.

The truth that God, the highest of all beings, identified
[Godself] with the lowest people, sharing their hardship and
suffering, is definitely the richest source of encouragement.
(P. 133)

Equality with God. As he did on the night he was first
arrested in Philippi, Paul uses a hymn to witness to
Christ's life of sacrifice and obedience as a source of encouragement. The material in this hymn may go back to
the images from the Suffering Servant hymn in Isa. 52:13
to 53:12, or to a song of praise out of the Hellenistic or
Jewish traditions. Here it is clearly a doxology to Christ
and to the actions of God in Jesus Christ, and may have
been sung at the Lord's Supper, or at Baptism. In any
case it has been incorporated by Paul into his letter as
the example of One who became God's instrument of divine help, through his refusal to crave "equality with
God" (Phil. 2:6). The "mind" of Christ which the Philippian church is to share is the desire to know and serve
God rather than the desire to promote selfish interests.
Because of God's action in Christ the New Creation has
begun in which human beings can live their lives as partners, serving one another.

The action of God in Christ is described in the two parts
of the hymn. Verses 6–8 tell of Christ's descent from divine glory. Like the first human being, Adam, this Second
Adam is in the image of God (Gen. 1:26–28). Yet, unlike
the first Adam, Christ does not grasp at his position of
privilege (I Cor. 15:45–47; Rom. 5:12–21). Rather, he takes
the form of human beings who are enslaved to demonic
powers and principalities (Gal. 4:1–9; Wayne Meeks). As
suffering servant, Christ is obedient to God's will even
when it leads to confrontation of these powers and to
death on the cross. Philippians 2:9–11 describe the way in
which obedience and humility are rewarded by God, who
lifts up the servant as Lord to receive the glory and praise
of all creation (Isa. 45:23; Rev. 4:11; 5:12).

Paul's hymn to Christ is a doxology not dissimilar to Psalm 8 in structure, telling of gracious deeds in the context of praise. It also has many of the same themes, but here in the hymn we hear that Christ was able to be a truly human person, able to glorify God in showing God's humanity to us. It is not surprising that the early Christian church called Jesus "Lord," for he was identified with God's will and purpose (I Cor. 12:3; Rev. 19:16). The word *doulos* ("slave," "servant") was always coupled with the word *kyrios* ("Lord") because it was this startling history of incarnation and resurrection that was the beginning of new humanity. Because he was willing to be *less than human* in the form of a slave, Jesus also became *more than human,* and those who called him Lord belonged to him and not to Caesar or to any human or demonic authority.

TRUE HUMANITY

It is no wonder that Paul used a hymn to celebrate the great mystery of Christ's humanity and divinity. It seems better to speak in metaphors of praise, celebrating the mystery of God's action, than to try to settle the question that Mary asked the angel Gabriel, "How can this be?" In our earnestness to pin things down we try to codify the angel chorus and the letters from prison. But, as Calvin said, even the creeds of the church should be sung lest they be misunderstood as defining God. In truth we cannot say *why* Jesus is truly human and truly divine. We can only celebrate our faith that he is, and then go on to tell the story of what he did. It is the story of Jesus, not the creeds, that makes God's action plausible. In the words of Dorothee Soelle,

I don't as they put it believe in god
but to him I can't say no
as hard as I try. (P. 16)

Jesus' Story. The story of Jesus is what is behind the titles
used by the early Christian church to praise his name.
Here in the Philippian hymn the imagery of the heavenly
representative who does his work through obedient suffering is brought together with the title of *Lord.* That title
rests on the story of his life and resurrection. Jesus is risen
and he continues to exercise the power of his love in the
church and the world until the New Age of liberation is
completed. The earthly Jesus was called "my Lord" or
"Master" during his life, and after the resurrection he was
called "the Lord" to signify his victory over sin and death
and his continuing unity with God as risen Lord. The word
kyrios ("lord") was a natural title to use of a god or a ruler
in Greek. It was used to translate the name of God, *Yahweh,* in the Greek Old Testament.

Jesus' title of *Servant* reflects his ministry in the service of God's kingdom. The Servant of Yahweh was an
image used in Second Isaiah to refer to the vicarious representation and suffering of God's servant (Isa. 42:1–9).
The Gospels tell Jesus' story as one of suffering service by
a man who called himself *Son of man* (Mark 8:38; 9:9;
14:62; Matt. 19:28). During the time of Jesus this term
was used to denote a pre-existent divine person who
would appear at the last days, or a pre-existent divine
person who was identical with the first person at creation. Jesus' ministry was also one of fulfillment of this
messianic role as the bringer of God's kingdom. Paul's
use of the image of the *Second Adam* reflects this background as he speaks of Jesus Christ as the heavenly representative who does his work through obedient suffering. In Rom. 5:12–21 he elaborates on the analogy
between the first human being and the second human

being and how our destiny is linked to their actions of
disobedience and obedience.

> For as by one [person's] disobedience many were made
> sinners, so by one [person's] obedience many will be made
> righteous. (Rom. 5:19)

This image of new humanity and the story of obedience
are crucial to us as we seek out what God intends for us.
This intention is rooted, not in a mythical human being
who never existed, or even in the many images or titles for
the One truly human being. God's intention for obedient
partnership in the work of New Creation is most clearly
seen not in a myth but in one man. For by God's intention
his story is a new beginning for the human story.

Lord and Servant. In Jesus' ministry, Lordship and Servanthood were together in the "establishment of justice
through suffering" (James Cone). The symbols of slavery or
servanthood, so often used in the New Testament, continue to evoke strong images and experiences of domination and involuntary subordination. Yet the scandal of
the words is at the heart of the gospel story (Matt. 23:11).
The Lord who voluntarily became a servant, who suffered
out of love for others, has called us to do likewise. As Hans
Hoekendijk has put it:

> Everything done by this Son of Man (Mark 10:45), who came
> to serve, including humiliation, self emptying, *cross,* death
> is summarized in one final communiqué of eight letters:
> *diakonia.* (P. 30)

In a world where so many people are enslaved, it is
difficult to understand the way service and power go together. We don't understand how it is that Christ is Lord
and Servant, and we certainly don't understand what that
would mean in our lives, in spite of Paul's "encouragement." For those who see themselves as victims of involuntary servitude because of racism, classism, sexism,
and the many isms of our world, talk of humility is "cheap

talk" especially when the ones doing the talking are those in positions of power and affluence. For those who see creation and its creatures as victims of domination, talk of dominion is "cheap talk," especially when the talkers live in a nation able to destroy the world many times over. Jesus' story seems to be part of the problem, in keeping some folks "down" and excusing the power of others.

But that is not what the Gospels tell us. They tell us that the Lord is Servant and that the Servant is Lord. The clue here seems to be that God's intention is that both empowerment and service should be part of our lives. In fact, the good news according to Mary is that in Christ, God

> . . . has put down the mighty from their thrones,
> and exalted those of low degree.
>
> (Luke 1:52)

This does not eliminate the dynamics of power in our lives. Power is the ability to accomplish desired ends, and without it there would be no life. What it does is recognize that in the Old Creation power and service have been falsely separated from each other. God's remedial work in restoring justice has to do with the need for that balance or partnership in all of creation.

According to God's intention we are to live in community in such a way that we can be subjects of our own destiny, yet also servants with those who share that destiny. When Christ is present in our midst, this sometimes happens in small anticipations of God's intended partnership. We notice the multiplying effect of mutual service. The whole becomes greater than the sum of the parts as gifts multiply and people are empowered by God's Spirit.

In reflecting on one such experience in my own life I noticed that empowerment and service seemed to be right at the heart of the experience of koinonia. At an ecumenical meeting in which I participated there was more than the usual "Pentecostal experience" of discover-

ing common language and common journey. The reason
for this seems to have been that there was an unusual level
of teamwork or partnership. Because of lack of staff and
funds, the same people, including myself, were responsible for program as well as for all the conference mainte-
nance tasks: moderating sessions and cleaning tables, lead-
ing discussions and typing documents. As we shared
together in both leadership and service, the gifts multiplied and there was an experience of wholeness and unity
in our human relationships.

The Power and the Glory

"For thine is the kingdom and the power and the glory
. . ." is the doxology that has been used by many Christian
churches at the close of the Lord's Prayer from earliest
times (Matt. 6:9–13; I Chron. 29:11). Even though Jesus'
words do not seem to have included this final word of
praise, it is not surprising that such a traditional Jewish
doxology was added as Christian communities recalled the
words of the Lord (Phil. 2:11). The affirmation of this doxology and of the hymn in Philippians 2 is that in Jesus
Christ Christians have discovered God's power and glory,
and seen it lived out *on earth* as in heaven.

But how is it lived out? How does glory look on earth?
A modern clue to this search can be seen in Graham
Greene's 1940 novel about religious persecution in Mexico
entitled *The Power and the Glory.* The martyr-priest is
much "too human for heroism and too humble for martyr-
dom." The story seems to reveal squalor and suffering, not
glory. It shows weakness and persecution, not power. Yet
this is what power and glory seem to look like from the
perspective of Calvary hill. Not only do they have a very
ordinary human face, they even have the face of those
marginal people that the world would call "nobodies."

The Human Story. In the light of the stark reality of the

cross it is difficult to avoid the fact that the real scandal is not just servanthood or humiliation. The real scandal is suffering. The human story is full of suffering in all its concrete reality as intense pain, both physical and social. It is a scandal that the story seems to reveal so much suffering but does not wipe it out of our lives immediately. And suffering remains very much with us, in many phases and dimensions, as Dorothee Soelle points out in her book on *Suffering* (pp. 70–74).

Our initial response to suffering in our lives is one of denial, speechlessness, and isolation. Even if we are not cut off from others in prison or hospital bed, or in the prison of pain itself, we tend to retreat into our own isolated world. Sometimes, however, we move through this to find a language in which to complain about our situation, lifting up our laments to God and to others around us. Finally we also may begin to confront the suffering itself, working to transform it or to live in and through it together with others. God's power and glory are present in our human condition no matter what the dimension of our suffering, because in Christ's suffering God has chosen to stand with us. Yet when we look to see this power and glory in human life, it shines through most clearly in those whose lives are confronting the suffering by saying *no* to its dehumanizing power.

One of the clearest expressions of this, with which most of us are familiar, is to be seen in the context of suffering and death experienced in hospitals. Patients in hospitals usually are lying there asking themselves, *Why me?* They are angry with God, with their own bodies, and are unwilling to accept the fact that they are sick or injured. Those who are around them as family, friends, clergy, or health care teams can't answer their questions. In fact, they can't even answer their own questions. These questions are often unspoken, but they are nevertheless real questions: *Why not me?* Why didn't I get sick? When will I get sick?

If it is a loved one, the "well persons" may feel guilty that
it is not they who are sick instead and at the same time feel
resentful that the patient has disrupted their lives.

In the middle of this isolation and questioning on every
side, an amazing thing often happens. Patients and nonpa-
tients begin to ask, *Who, me, God?* and to take responsibility for their situation before God, seeking to live faithfully
in the midst of suffering. In this moment of recognizing
God's call in the midst of that situation the word of God's
power in Jesus Christ speaks to us in and through our
human story. That word of power is that nothing "in all
creation, will be able to separate us from the love of God"
(Rom. 8:39).

Power and Glory. Suffering is a sign of the kingdom of
God. Not only because we discover God's power in its
depth, but also because it is suffering in all its forms that
God opposes in the establishment of New Creation. In the
man Jesus, God asserts that the creation is to be put right.
In his story, suffering and death do their worst, and in that
story God is victorious over these powers so that we need
not be their slaves. According to Moltmann:

> The crucified Lord embodies the new humanity which re-
> sponds to God in the circumstances of inhumanity which
> oppose God. (P. 116)

Meanwhile, as we await our full liberation as children of
God, we know that our human life has hidden in its midst
the power and the glory of a God who cares enough to
suffer with us. Through this we know already that human
life is destined, not for suffering, but for partnership with
God: a partnership so strong that not even suffering can
break it; a partnership that will one day be fulfilled in the
New Creation where "the Lord GOD will wipe away tears
from all faces" (Isa. 25:8).

When God's Spirit breaks into our lives in small anticipations of this time of glory, we suddenly discover that we

are *somebody,* but not because of anything we have done or any "S/N degree" that we have earned. We are somebody because we have accepted the presence in our lives of the One who calls us partner. It is in this and this only that we can glory, that our humanity is more than human because God has chosen to become a *nobody* and to share our humanity with us.

5
HUMAN NATURE
Genesis 1:26–30; 2:18–24

As the congregation gathered to worship God they noticed something out of the ordinary. Above the chancel steps a large white sheet was hung so that they could no longer see the Communion table and the cross. It looked as though the sermon was going to be replaced with a "picture show." But nothing new seemed to happen. At the appropriate time the Scripture from Genesis 2 was read and the sermon on "Creation" began. Slowly, however, the words seemed to take shape. First, little marks on the sheet, then larger shapes, then a human form, and then another. Pretty soon unseen brushstrokes had brought God's creatures together, dancing in pairs at first and then all joined in one circle of life. It was a little difficult to listen to the sermon as the figures drew the congregation's attention. Then the next stage of creation appeared before their eyes: the dark brushstrokes of the unseen painter gradually changed the circle of life into the crown of thorns. The congregation waited. Was there more to come?

This is the question we ask the writers of a prelude to history in Genesis 1–3. Of course we know the answer. There is more to come, the entire history of God's dealing with humanity, a history of disobedience, thorns, and promise. Having looked at the other end of that promised

60

future as it shapes the intention for our lives in the *present*, we turn now to ask what this prelude tells us about our *origin*. Who are we as man and woman created by God? What was God up to in the first place when we were shaped into a circle of life? How are we to understand our human nature?

Like the parables of the kingdom of God, the stories of this prehistory in Genesis 1–11 intend to tell us something about God's reality as it contrasts with the way things are. The stories speak in metaphors and hints of God's creative work, but very clearly of the human disobedience and resulting dislocation of creation that produced "thorns and thistles" (3:18). The problem, however, is not in the poetic descriptions of the mystery of our beginnings, but in the assumption that we can turn the stories into blueprints for life—orders of creation that never can change.

As a prologue to the history of God's liberating actions on behalf of Israel and of humankind, the stories do not provide *conclusions* to what life is all about, but rather *clues* for Israel's journey as it begins with God's call to Abraham and Sarah in Genesis 12. As with other journeys, it is important to know your destination, but once that is decided, past experience of your starting point may provide valuable clues about how to get there. Thus we join the writers of Israel's prehistory in remembering the clues for our future out of the past.

MALE AND FEMALE

In Genesis 1 and 2 we have two different descriptions of the way in which the liberating God of the Hebrew people was also the creating God of all humankind and of the whole earth. The Bible as it comes to us today is a combination of many sources and traditions put together by various editors. In the case of the creation story, two versions have been placed side by side to complement each other. Genesis 1 is a product of theological reflection by later editors from the time after the exile in Babylon who are usually known as the Priestly writers. Genesis 2 and 3 reflect the views of an early editor or editors from the time of King David, usually called the Yahwist.

So God Created Them. The climax of the Priestly narrative of creation is found in Gen. 1:26–30. Beginning with the element most distant from God, the powers of chaos, the writers finally reach the beings closest to God. Male and female are created in the image of God and have dominion over the other parts of creation. The plural of divine deliberation in v. 26 may reflect the idea of discussion in a heavenly court, or may be a plural of majesty like that used by heads of state. The word used for God, *Elohim,* is plural, but it is regularly used in Hebrew as a singular name. The plural origin may reflect the male and female gods of the Near Eastern pantheon whose characteristics are both included and transcended by Israel's God. In any case the words "Let us make . . ." serve to prevent the reader from assuming that the image is a direct representation of God (3:22). It also points toward v. 27, where God carries out creation of male and female in God's image.

Verses 28–30 are again in the first person as God blesses woman and man. Like the animals, they are to be fruitful and multiply and to eat only plants. But, unlike the animals, they and their descendants are to have dominion over creation. Scholars do not agree on the amount of emphasis to be placed on the specification of human creation as male and female. But whether this is an important bearer of the metaphor of the image of God (Phyllis Trible), or whether it is only included in v. 27 to specify the biological basis for blessing in v. 28 (Phyllis Bird), it is clear that both sexes bear the image of God and share in God's blessing. The customary English translation of *'adam* in v. 27 as "man" rather than as "humankind" is inaccurate, and leads to the false conclusion that if man is in God's image, God must be masculine.

Not Lonesome but Twosome. The Yahwist tells a different story of creation in Gen. 2:4b–24. The ancient creation myths of the Near East have been woven together skillfully to present God, called *Yahweh* (LORD in the RSV), as the sole source of life and creation. Here human creatures are also the focus of attention, but the story places them in the center of a circle of relationships with God, plants, and animals, rather than at the pinnacle of a pyramid, as in the Priestly account (Gerhard von Rad).

The story of human creation begins in vs. 7–8 with a pun on the word *'adam* which is similar to the word for earth *('adama). The human* (earth creature) is formed by Yahweh out of *the earth.* It is not yet either male or female but simply, like the animals, a living creature formed from earth and filled with God's breath (vs. 7, 19). After creating a garden of trees where the earth creature can dwell and work (vs. 9–17), Yahweh creates the animals, hoping they will be companions for the human (vs. 18–20). As Phyllis Trible explains:

> The earth creature needs a companion, one who is neither subordinate nor superior, one who alleviates isolation through identity. (P. 90)

The last act and climax of this creation sequence is the creation of human sexuality (vs. 21–24). Instead of using earth as raw material as with the earth creature and the animals, Yahweh uses the flesh of the earth creature to create woman. In the process of God's act, the living being becomes a man and a woman. The joy of the man, underlined in the pun on the Hebrew words for woman *(ishsha)* and man *(ish)* in v. 23, is expressed as delight at what God had done in creating sexuality (Phyllis Trible). The man does not *name* the woman as he did the animals. It is only later (in ch. 3:20), after the Fall, that she is named Eve by one called Adam. Verse 24 confirms this mutual belonging as man recognizes that his desire is for physical oneness with her.

Whereas the Priestly writer has emphasized human sexuality in relation to the blessing of fertility and dominion of the descendants, the Yahwist culminates the description of created harmony with the fulfillment, not just of biological community but also of social partnership (Phyllis Bird). To be created by God as woman and man was to be "not lonesome but twosome," and was to find human wholeness in community.

IMAGE OF GOD

Whenever we begin to examine the creation stories for clues to the nature of human beings, we are caught up in the excitement of discovering what may be clues to a usable past for our journey toward self-understanding. But in the next moment we find ourselves caught fast in the conflicting interpretations and misinterpretations. Over the ages, our search for understanding of who we are as God's creatures has always returned to cause us to look in the "mirror of man and woman" found in these famous texts. Looking in the glass, people see themselves and their own context and call it "God." But God is not in the mirror and remains free of our pretensions. The stories somehow seem to call all the various definitions of God's image into question.

Image and Dominion. The myth of *man* created in the image of God and exercising dominion over the earth has been used over and over to justify the domination over women and other subordinate groups as well as over creation itself. It is no exaggeration to say that all these people have been, and are, the victims of a myth. Yet a study of the *image* in Genesis 1 does not support such views. The text indicates only that there is some unspecified resem-

blance between male and female and God (1:27). The use
of the parallel term "likeness," or similarity, along with
"image" in v. 26 serves, not to explain its meaning, but
rather to keep the meaning as unspecific as possible and
preserve the freedom of God.

The image itself eludes us when we press it beyond the
writers' intention of saying that somehow God is uniquely
represented in creation by human beings. This should not
surprise us, because, although the background of the word
for image refers to "plastic work, duplicate, or idol," it is
used here to describe more than an appearance (Gerhard
von Rad). Perhaps we could say that the image has to do
with the totality of the human person in relation to God,
and as such is not reducible to one or another quality such
as rationality, spirituality, or even sexuality. Its meaning is
mainly to be seen in the action that follows from it, that
of having dominion over the earth.

The references to *dominion* in Gen. 1:26 and 28 indicate that human beings are to be God's representatives in
caring for creation. As was mentioned in the discussion of
Psalm 8 in Chapter 3, the two ideas of image and dominion
may reflect a royal ideology of the ancient Near East that
a king is enthroned as the ruler over the land as a representative and image of a god. In this sense the king is
understood as a living idol of the god. The designation of
task to humanity in Gen. 1:28–30 still seems to retain this
idea of governing, ruling, and mastery over the rest of
creation, according to Phyllis Bird (Ps. 8:7).

Although the command, "Be fruitful and multiply, and
fill the earth" is included along with the command to subdue the earth and have dominion, this is not directly a part
of the image relationship (Gen. 1:28). The same command
is given to the other creatures, and reproduction is not
uniquely human (v. 22). The only difference is that here
procreation will have the effect of not only filling but also
subduing the earth and carrying forward the history of

God's covenant partnership with Israel (Genesis 11). Although humanity is understood to be male and female by the Priestly writers, their imagery reflects a patriarchal understanding of human order.

Sexuality and Human Community. The Yahwist account in Genesis 2 also reflects the cultural assumptions of male dominance, but in a critical way. Man and woman are created twosome for the purpose of human community and companionship, not for the purpose of procreation. The relationship of the earth creature to the plant and animal world is one of caring and tending, not of subordination. In fact, the Yahwist presents domination over the woman and over the earth as punishment for human disobedience in ch. 3:16–17. Before the Fall, man and woman are to be companions together, finding joy in union with each other.

This earlier creation narrative gives us clues to human nature in relation to God, but does not use the words *image* and *dominion* to describe that nature. Nor is there any differentiation of roles between man and woman before their disobedience. A possible exception to this is that the woman is described as the more intelligent and more prominent than the man in the first part of ch. 3 in poetic contrast to her subordination in the punishment that follows.

Human sexuality, recognized by the Priestly writer as part of the image, is here held up as a metaphor for relationship between fellow human beings. This sexuality may be expressed through sexual intercourse, but it stretches far beyond that. Human sexuality refers to a whole range of behaviors that go into our makeup as male and female. It is an ever-evolving sense of our self-identity as man or woman, rooted in but not determined by our biological sex (Letty Russell, *The Future of Partnership*, p. 82). As an expression of who we are as a totality of spirit and body in relation to others, sexuality can provide metaphors for our relationship to God and God's relationship to us.

As Phyllis Trible has documented in her fascinating book on *God and the Rhetoric of Sexuality,* the use of the metaphor of sexuality comes into play not only in the creation narratives but also in other parts of the Old Testament. Both masculine and feminine images are used to portray the way God relates to human beings and their concerns. Female imagery such as that of the womb suggests what Trible calls a natural and spontaneous relationship between the divine and the human rather than one of rights and law, and it embodies God's intimate embrace (Isa. 49:15; Ps. 22:9–10). The range of images helps us to express a full range of capacity for relationship between ourselves and God, and one another.

Paul Jewett in *Man as Male and Female* suggests that theologians have interpreted human sexuality and the image of God in three ways (pp. 23–48). Some have argued that humanity originally had the characteristics of both sexes. This view that the human creature was created both male and female and then was separated into two halves is not substantiated at all by Genesis 1, nor by the Yahwist account, where the earth creature has no sexuality (not two sexualities) until the creation of companions (Phyllis Trible).

Other theologians have ignored human sexuality in discussing the creation stories, claiming that it is not important for understanding the image. The result is that the relationship of male and female is discussed only in the context of marriage, procreation, and sexual sin, and anthropology is reduced to a discussion of the *male* as human.

A third interpretation, developed by Dietrich Bonhoeffer and Karl Barth, is that the male and female distinctions are grounded in the image of God. As we have seen,

this interpretation is helpful for underlining the interrela-
tion between human beings and God and between each
other. Most biblical scholars do not think that Genesis 1
supports this view, although Phyllis Trible argues very
persuasively that in the metaphor of image in v. 27 the
words "male and female" are "the finger pointing to the
'image of God' " (p. 20). Barth links human sexuality to the
concept of an unchangeable ordering of creation estab-
lished by God. Thus he asserts that the male/female dis-
tinction is an unchangeable order of relationship in which
man is always *A* and woman is always *B* according to God's
command (pp. 217–219). This seems closer to the description of "the way it is" after the Fall than of God's intention
for partnership.

HELPER FIT FOR HIM

Ultimately it is not possible to establish one single interpretation of the metaphor of image. This ambiguity of
meaning and confusion of interpretation is already present in the biblical materials, let alone in the later traditions. In biblical and church tradition the problems in
understanding image, dominion, and sexuality have often
led to a form of self-fulfilling prophecy. In their personal
and communal histories, people of faith have tended to be
shaped by misinterpretations of these images of origin.

It is this sort of process that is at work, for instance, in
Paul's famous passage about why women should be veiled
when preaching (I Cor. 11:2–16). In a church where the
Spirit had broken out, Paul struggles to present the old
order of "headship" in creation (v. 3). Drawing on Jewish
tradition, Paul interprets the image of God by using the
Yahwist story. He claims that it is man who gives God glory
by reflecting the image of God, but not the woman, who
is a reflection of the man (v. 7)! Yet Paul has to admit that
in Christ man and woman are not independent (vs. 11–12).

Paul is able to correct his understanding as he looks toward Christ and God's intention for the New Creation (II Cor. 5:16–21). In the same way, we have to be critical of what is read into the stories of origin in the light of God's intention for partnership with us. In this perspective we may want to de-emphasize the understanding of dominion and to reemphasize the understanding of helper or companion.

Pinnacle of the Pyramid. As we saw, the Priestly version presents human beings at the "pinnacle of the pyramid" of creation. This "royalty ideology" is somewhat modified by inclusion of all men and, possibly, women at the top along with the kingly representative. When the image of God is understood in this way our perception of reality tends to be limited to the "view from the top." We forget that God is also the creator and sustainer of all the subordinated persons and parts of creation. Our responsibility as partners and stewards with God is obscured in the need to maintain a very insecure position above the rest. This way of looking at the world, when combined with human disobedience, becomes a temptation to be *man as ruler*. It was just this temptation that Jesus rejected in Luke 4:1–12. He refused to exercise power from the "pinnacle of the temple" to dominate and manipulate people or kingdoms.

The image of *God as helper* is much closer to Jesus' understanding of God's action in his life. God is understood as the one who has solidarity with humanity and in this suffering and redeeming action exercises power. The image of helper, or paraclete, in the New Testament is very powerful. For instance, Paul in Phil. 2:1 begins his appeal for humility and unity with an appeal to the help or "encouragement in Christ." John's Gospel speaks of the Holy Spirit as the paraclete, the one who helps, encourages, and upbuilds. The paraclete is literally someone who stands at our side and advocates our cause. In the psalms and elsewhere in the Old Testament, God is frequently referred to as "a very present help in trouble" (Ps. 46:1). In Ps. 63:1–8 God's power and glory are revealed through covenant faithfulness and help:

> For you have been my helper and under the shadow of your wings I will rejoice. (Tr. by Keith Watkins, cf. pp. 30–47)

It would seem that the image of God needs to come down from the pinnacle and share the humanity of God.

Circle of Relationships. The Yahwist account reflects more of this view of reality as it presents human beings in the center of a circle of relationships among the divine, human, animal, and plant worlds. According to Von Rad, "solitude" is defined as "helplessness," because human beings are created to live in community.

Recognizing the earth creature's need for "a helper fit for him," God creates animals, but they are unsuitable partners because of the relationship of subordination which is underlined in the naming process. So then God creates woman as helper. The translation of the Hebrew word *ezer* as helper has led to a great deal of misunderstanding because it is assumed that this means that woman is man's subordinate. In fact, its meaning is the opposite of this, for the word is frequently used in the Hebrew scriptures to describe God's helping action. As Trible points out, the accompanying phrase "fit for him" or "corresponding to him" is necessary to show that the intention is not that woman be superior, like God, but rather one who shares "identity, mutuality and equality" (p. 90).

The act of creating woman and man is *an act of creating helpers* who are companions for each other. It fulfills the need for life-in-community. As God is partner to humanity, men and women are to be partner to one another. The rights of human beings as those created to represent God are also the responsibilities of human beings as those created for relationship. When we separate these two aspects of our human nature, and assign "rights" to males and "responsibilities" to females, we fall short of the common humanity that we share together. To give glory to God by representing God before others is to exercise dominion as a gracious neighbor, sharing God's help as helpers of others.

The story of our origins is not the only word on human nature. By beginning from the other end, we already know that we share in God's image because of the humanity of God. In God's action in Jesus Christ we can see that the God who created us *to need help* and *to help* is also the God who has become our Helper. God's help is offered to us as a gift, in spite of the fact that we are helpers who have fallen short of the glory of God and have refused to be "radically helped" (Karl Barth).

6
LESS THAN HUMAN
Genesis 2:25 to 3:24

We might search for a long time to find a community of persons where there are a few small signs of hope that it is possible for human beings to share in helping others and in being helped. But we don't have to look beyond the front page of the newspaper to discover signs of less-than-human activity. There are people who degrade and destroy others, whose behavior is "a little lower than the animals." There are the "others" who barely survive as human persons in a world that punishes the poor and sick, and blames the victims.

The battered woman is one example of these countless victims of personal and social sin. Her silent screams cry out to us from isolation, fear, and pain even when we cannot hear her actual screams. The battered woman is caught in a circle of violence which she is powerless to break on her own. She finds herself blamed as "neurotic," as "unfaithful," as "masochistic," as anything except a victim of violence from the man to whom she looks for protection and love. Her husband, himself victimized by his ego needs to prove himself, punishes her for his misery. She sees herself as a failure because she is unable to maintain the "mythical" nuclear family as a center of safety and comfort, and, in fear, cuts herself off from what little help she might find in community or church. The man wants to show that he *doesn't need help,* all the while enslaving the woman as his "helper." The woman wants to show that she is helpless and dependent, and *does need help,* all the while acting as helper.

Looked at from the perspective of this less-than-human situation, the Genesis 3 account of human disobedience and dislocation of relationships reads like a newspaper editorial on our contemporary society. As described by Phyllis Trible, the consequences of human disobedience in the Yahwist story of the Fall even sound like the "battered woman syndrome":

> Where once there was mutuality, now there is a hierarchy of division. The man dominates the woman to pervert sexuality. Hence, the woman is corrupted in becoming a slave, and the man is corrupted in becoming a master. (P. 128)

Before us in Genesis 3 we find the story of human alienations skillfully woven together, not only to explain why things are as they are but also to explain that they were once otherwise and can be so again.

HIS WIFE'S NAME EVE

When it comes to biblical tradition, the answer to the question, "What's in a name?" is, "A whole lot!" For the naming of God, persons, animals, and places has a great deal of significance. According to ancient ideas a name was not just "noise and smoke" (Ex. 3:1–15; Gerhard von Rad). The subject was in the name, and to know the name was to know the subject. Name-giving was understood as an exercise in authority and command. Thus the naming of the animals in Gen. 2:19–20 is not only an indication of the human ability to organize the world and to understand it by means of language but also an indication of dominion over the animals.

As we saw in the discussion of human nature in Chapter

5, the creation of woman corresponding to man, and thus able to be helper with him, led to joyous welcome but not to naming (2:23). Although v. 23 in the RSV says, "she shall be called Woman," the Hebrew phrase for naming employs the word "name" along with "called" (v. 11). When the man does name the woman, in ch. 3:20, it reads

> The man called his wife's name Eve, because she was the mother of all living.

According to Phyllis Trible, the result of human disobedience and dislocation is that the woman is no longer viewed as partner but as possession. Yet her name, Eve, is also a sign of grace. She is to be the mother of life in a world which is under the threat of death.

Helping Themselves. The first scene of the Yahwist's creation story in ch. 2:7–24 presents human beings as helpers who are being helped by God and by each other. But having shown the way things should be, the writer moves quickly to the account of the temptation and fall in 2:25 to 3:7. In helping themselves to the fruit of the tree of all knowledge, the couple disobey God's command and refuse to be helped by God.

The occasion for the disobedience is one of the animals. Created to be a help to human beings, the serpent now becomes a "helper" who hurts (Phyllis Trible). With God absent from the scene, the woman discusses theology with the serpent, making clear her knowledge of God's command given to the earth creature (2:15–17). The woman decides to transgress God's command in order to become wise. The man is with her throughout the entire scene, and his sin is presented as one of passive complicity, an accomplice in disobedience. The mutuality of the disobedience is hidden in the RSV because of the omission of the Hebrew phrase "who was with her" in ch. 3:6. The text says, ". . . and she gave some to her husband *who was with her* and he ate" (Cheryl Exum).

The knowledge that the couple gain is a recognition of their own defenselessness and guilt. In fear and shame at their helplessness they try to cover their bodies. Having refused the radical help and merciful care of God, they now hide from God behind their fig leaves and the trees of the garden.

Fallen Reality. The final scene and climax of the Yahwist's story is the description of the resulting dislocation and punishment in which one partner becomes a "helpmate" and the other goes on struggling to help himself (3:8–24). The trial of the man, woman, and serpent is especially interesting because of the way it foreshadows the judgment by indicating the fracture of relationships that already exists (vs. 8–13). The man betrays and blames the woman, and then blames God for giving him the woman, before he confesses his disobedience. The woman blames the serpent, and speaking only for herself says, ". . . and I ate."

The judgment on the serpent, the woman, and the man makes use of the experience of human misery and sin in the author's own Israelite culture (vs. 14–19). Yet the profundity and accuracy of this description is underlined by the fact that it still speaks to us today in our situations as "battered persons." The animal world is portrayed in a power struggle with the descendants of Eve, each seeking to kill the other. While the serpent is to eat the dust from which it was created, man is to return to that dust, having struggled with the earth to wrestle life from its thorns and thistles. The woman will share man's pain and suffering, but hers will be multiplied in the suffering of childbirth and of desiring reunion with a partner who instead has become her master. In a sense the woman "falls down," while the man, in perversion of his created nature, "falls up" (Elizabeth Dodson Gray).

The close of the story indicates the depth of alienation and dislocation (vs. 20–24). Human sexuality is now a model for the domination of one partner over the other. The vulnerability of man and woman in needing each other has to be protected by the provision of clothing. God does not pronounce a *curse* except on the serpent and the ground, but vs. 22–24 indicate the punishment which follows from what Adam and Eve have already done to themselves. Death will place a limit on the pretension and disobedience of the ones who no longer belong in a garden of life.

In this tragic story we find a variety of answers to the question, "What is man?" According to Phyllis Trible, the word *'adam* is used three ways in the texts, although this is difficult to discern in translation. Until the helper is created, *'adam* is a sexually undifferentiated earth creature. When humanity becomes male and female, *'adam* is the word used to designate humanity as *male*. But subsequent to the act of naming *his* woman, Eve, *'adam* becomes a generic term that "keeps the man visible and the woman invisible" (Gen 3:22–24; pp. 134–135). Man is still human, but what is the woman? Less than human?

REFUSAL TO BE RADICALLY HELPED

The Priestly writers have no story of the Fall. Instead, they picture a gradual loss of human perfection as the length of years of life grows shorter and shorter (Genesis 5). The Fall is a gradual decline until God's intervention through Noah and the Flood leads to a covenant with creation (6:11–18). The Yahwist, on the other hand, presents us with a sudden breaking of relationships which is followed by further spread of sin across the face of the earth, climaxing with the story of the tower of Babel (11: 1–9).

Broken Relationship. One thing all the sources do agree on is that human beings were created as God's earth creatures, finite or limited by their creaturely existence yet with freedom to transcend that existence in responsibility for others before God. This ability to transcend ourselves and our physical existence is the basis of our freedom, but is also the basis of our disobedience. Created able to go beyond ourselves in relation to others, we could also use this same self-transcendence to break off our relationship to God and to others. It is as though we were created in a dancing circle of life. In choosing to turn away from God we also have to break the handclasp with our dancing companions (Donald Baillie, in Fackre, p. 78).

In trying to explain how we could be cut off from God, our neighbors, and ourselves, some theologians such as Thomas Aquinas have spoken of the *lost* image of God. Distinguishing between the parallel words "image" and "likeness" in Gen. 1:26, they said that human beings retained the image or their natural ability to reason and to choose, but lost the "likeness" which consists of supernatural gifts for living in harmony with God. In the Roman Catholic view the gifts could be restored through the grace of God mediated in the Sacraments of the church. Protestant reformers such as Martin Luther and John Calvin held that Scripture spoke of only one image, and that image has been corrupted or lost. Our reason and ability to choose was so corrupted that only God's free gift of grace in Jesus Christ was able to restore the possibility of obedience and harmony with God and neighbor.

If we were to discuss what has happened to the image of God using the Old Testament view of human nature described in Chapter 5, it would seem that it would be better to ask what happened to the divine command to "have dominion," rather than to try to figure out if that which is very difficult to find is lost (Gen. 1:26). The command to have dominion over the earth is a command to represent God before all beings, letting God's glory be seen in graciousness to all creation.

In the denial of human dependence on God, and the

refusal to live according to God's intention for human life, three things happen. Representation becomes *replacement*, dominion becomes *domination*, and self-transcendence becomes *trespass*. Instead of being responsible before God as representatives, human beings seek to replace God with their own knowledge and power, so that creaturely dependence on God is denied. Dominion becomes domination of the creation and of other persons. The human ability to transcend self in relation to others in community is turned into a circle of trespass used to prove human self-importance, worth, and independence.

In Genesis 3 we see this broken relationship spelled out in a story of the fracture of social community. In disobeying, the man and the woman try to "play God," thus ending up unable to represent God as stewards of the garden. Dominion is replaced by domination as man struggles to subdue the earth and becomes master over the woman. The gender identity or sexuality of the human beings ceases to be a way of expressing self-transcending love, interdependence, and mutuality. It becomes an occasion not only for subordination but also for establishment of fixed masculine and feminine gender roles within which women and men struggle to express what is now only a partial form of humanity.

The loss of the image of God is not, in my opinion, the loss of any one capacity. Rather, it is the *perversion of the very things we do best.* Man's stereotyped role of domination and woman's stereotyped role of mother have become the vehicle for *both* woman and man to become less than human.

Sin as Occasion for Sin. The many ways that sin has been understood in Christian theology are themselves an occasion for further sin. Often religious authorities have named certain things as "sin," and people as "sinners," and ignored other obvious personal and social fractures.

This is one way of putting a "hedge" around responsibility to God, and trying to limit complicity in sin.

Yet the basic view of sin in the Old Testament does not allow us to reduce sin into any one sector of our lives or any one action. Sin is understood as a breakdown of the covenant relationship caused by disobedience. Hebrew words that are frequently translated "sin" in English have meanings such as missing the mark, rebellion or violation of the covenant, and disobedience. Here the emphasis is on the social aspect of sin, pointing to Israel's denial of responsible obedience to a God who had delivered them from slavery (Jer. 31:31–34).

In the New Testament, sin is still understood in the context of the faith community, and it continues to be understood as a denial of covenant through actions of injustice. In the writings of Paul the emphasis is on sin as lack of faith. One "misses the mark" by refusing to have a relationship of trust with God in Jesus Christ. In the light of the gospel, sin is viewed as "hatred of God" and rejection of Jesus Christ (Rom. 8:7; 14:23).

In later church traditions sin takes on a quantitative aspect in relation to overcoming *sins* through participation in the life of the church. Here sin tends to be understood as the opposite of virtue, rather than of faith or covenant relationship. When sin is understood quantitatively it is possible to speak of each action separately and so add up one's debts and credits. The problem with this, however, is that preoccupation with personal sins may lead to forgetfulness about the source of those actions which is the broken relationship with God.

Perhaps the reason for these and many other reinterpretations of the Hebrew/Christian tradition is not just the need to incarnate the message in particular cultures and situations. It would seem that some of the reason flows from human sin itself. Like the first humans, we want to avoid responsibility for our disobedience and therefore cast blame in one or another direction. When it comes down to "the bottom line," however, there is no getting away from the fact that we all hide from God by seeking to limit our responsibility before God and our dependence on God. In spite of ourselves we would rather "help ourselves" than let God help us (Rom. 2:1–11).

This is what *refusal to be radically helped* is all about. Created dependent on God, yet free to exercise our representing function, we refuse that dependence on God's graciousness. Such grace or help is *radical* for two reasons. First, in the sense of getting back to the roots, the divine/ human relationship of dependent freedom is rooted in God's choice to be helper to humanity and to keep human life human. Secondly, in the sense of drastic action, radical help is needed for human beings to find their way back into the circle of humanity with other human beings and with God. Just how radical becomes more clear when we admit the depth and breadth of the power of sin in our lives, and recognize the price that God has paid for the restoration of creation.

STRUCTURES OF DOMINATION

The depth and breadth of human sin sometimes escapes us because we do not see that sin has a social reality that is the source of "bondage to decay" in all creation (Rom. 8:21). As Reinhold Niebuhr has pointed out in his classic work on *The Nature and Destiny of Man,* the Bible defines sin in both religious and moral terms.

> The religious dimension of sin is [human] rebellion against God, [the] effort to usurp the place of God. The moral and social dimension of sin is injustice. (Vol. I, p. 179)

The social dimension of sin, which results in injustice, is often called oppression.

Wretched Humanity. Oppression is not difficult to define for those who suffer its effects. They are very clear that "sin is *mortal*" (Jon Sobrino). Not only does oppression bring spiritual death, but its social results mean that oppressed people die every day from tyranny, murder, starvation, and disease. Oppression destroys the humanity of the oppressor groups because they perpetuate evil and it destroys the humanity of oppressed groups through their suffering (Jürgen Moltmann).

Social sin has a life of its own. It functions in social systems in such a way that people are battered and dehumanized in countless ways simply because society does business as usual. Those who, like Jesus, are about God's business, inevitably find themselves standing against such oppression as they work "to set at liberty those who are oppressed" (the crushed ones; Luke 4:18). The structures of oppression are supported by various forms of collective human sin such as racism, sexism, and classism. Such isms are manifestations of self-justification and self-pride mixed with inhuman anxiety. Individuals and groups are sacrificed to the human idols of pride that prop up a less-than-human ego by oppressing others.

The "root of all evil" is the *miscarried love of God* (Jürgen Moltmann and M. Douglas Meeks). We are created to love God, and when we love lesser "gods" our whole being is distorted (Rom. 1:18–22). This distortion takes many forms. Niebuhr reminds us, however, that there are two very basic aspects related to human finitude as creatures of God, and to freedom as representatives of God (Vol. I, p. 186). When we flee from our finitude and try to extend our freedom beyond human limitations, we fall "up to" pride. When we flee from our freedom and try to bury ourselves in the day-to-day activities of our existence and the immediate needs around us we fall "down to" sensuality (Judith Plaskow). Sin thus perpetuates structures of oppression actively in the infinite expansion of human pride, and passively in the willingness to be preoccupied with immediate needs while society continues to crush its victims.

What has been known as *original sin* in church tradition does not mean that sin is inevitable. It is universal but not necessary (Reinhold Niebuhr). Although we share in the original dislocation of creation, sin is not part of human destiny. It is part of our history and can be overcome by the God of history (Jürgen Moltmann). In order for us to recognize our part in the social as well as the personal forms of sin, it is necessary to correct the perception of sin and sins that has been inherited from Christian tradition.

Divided Humanity. In trying to identify and list human sins and devise ways of overcoming them, the early church theologians made interpretations that suited the world view of their own times and cultures but that have had disastrous results for many oppressed groups in society (Justo Gonzalez). In locating the image of God in the soul and intellect and dividing it from the "animal" body, they justified the superiority of those who were not tied to mundane bodily functions of life, such as women and slaves. Such persons were literally understood as less than human because of their bodily identity, although such a dualism of soul and body is foreign to the Genesis understanding of anthropology.

The privatization of sin compounded this effect, and the repercussions are still felt in our homes, churches, and society. Sins were reinterpreted as personal actions of unfaithfulness, usually related to the temptations of the body which dragged the soul into the "dust"! Sins of the body were in turn linked to sex and women. Today we find the biblical emphasis on justice for the poor and oppressed neglected in favor of emphasis on issues related to sexuality, such as abortion, marital infidelity, and homosexuality.

One way of regaining a more wholistic understanding of sin is to try to move beyond the stereotypes that project our responsibilities onto others. The divisions between body and soul, person and society, or any other such dualisms prevent us from seeing the whole picture of sin. They give us a false picture of human reality in which one whole interrelated life/body is related to all other parts of creation. All of us, both body and spirit, both person and society, both male and female, are included in broken relationships with God and with others, and not just part of us.

Dualistic stereotypes mask the actual differences in the way women and men experience sin in their lives. For men frequently experience sin at the point of their strength (independence, assertion of rights, domination over others). Women in turn then experience it at their point of strength (interdependence, assertion of responsibilities, subordination to others). To overcome these particular forms of broken relationship, attention needs to be given to the way men and women develop and to their particular ways of relating to the world so that each may receive the help that she or he needs (Carol Gilligan). Without this attention, stereotypes of the meaning of sin may lead to reinforcement of the actual problems being faced. For instance, Valerie Saiving has pointed out that women's greatest temptation is not so much the pride and will to power that besets many men, but rather lack of self-esteem and a willingness to remain weak (p. 37). Failure to recognize this is a form of collective social sin that results in such dehumanization as that of the battered woman.

When Julius Nyerere was president of Tanzania he said that the reason he wanted to work for social justice in his country was that all human beings are created in the image of God.

> I refuse to image a God who is miserable, poor, ignorant, superstitious, fearful, oppressed and wretched—which is the lot of the majority of those ... created in [God's] image. (*The Radical Bible*, p. 13)

The reality of our less-than-human world is that this is exactly what God does look like. God has taken the side of those who need God's help, and, here and there in their midst, there may be a moment when the helpers are radically helped. At least this seems to be the promise of Matt. 25:31–46, where Jesus tells us of his presence with the poor. In taking the side of those who need help, we too may discover the Help we need to become human!

7
HUMAN NURTURE
Galatians 5:1–26

Seated around the kitchen table in a public housing project, we were talking theology, although we didn't call it that! The children had settled down and three of us were hard at work. We had an important assignment. Some people from the World Council of Churches in Geneva had sent us a letter asking what salvation means in East Harlem. For many people in our multiracial ghetto of poverty it would mean the possibility of "coming out ahead" in their struggle for survival, perhaps hitting the numbers, or getting a job. For others it would mean religious revival or the heavenly music of a storefront Pentecostal church. For those of us seated at the table it was a big question.

How should we name the discovery of new life and hope? What did it mean in our experience? A few "conversion stories" later, one woman suddenly blurted out, "It means that I'm more free!" And that was that. We all agreed. In New York City, and in the year 1967, salvation had to mean *freedom*—freedom to hope in God, freedom to be human.

But how do we get free? How do we find that power of God's love which can unlock us from personal and social bondage? How do we nurture a human life of freedom? In a letter written to the Galatians, sometime around the

year 50, Paul answers this question with a long story con-
densed into only five Greek words: "For freedom Christ
has set us free" (Gal. 5:1). Christ is the one who sets us free
and it is to Christ that we look to find out what it would
mean to share in becoming human.

CHRIST HAS SET US FREE

Christians are not always happy to hear that *Jesus means
freedom* (Ernst Käsemann). But there is no ambiguity
about the gospel message in this regard. In Paul's letter to
the Galatians it is the central motif. The situation of Christian before God and before the world has been radically
transformed. Liberated from all that had been dislocated
through the Fall, they were now free to live in harmony
with God and one another.

> For as many of you as were baptized into Christ have put
> on Christ. There is neither Jew nor Greek, there is neither
> slave nor free, there is neither male nor female; for you are
> all one in Christ Jesus. (Gal. 3:27–28)

Writing to a church in Asia Minor during his missionary
travels in that region, Paul confronts those who have
"slipped in to spy out our freedom" to bring us back into
bondage (2:4). Apparently these visiting preachers were
"freedom haters." They wanted "law and order" in the
form of following the Jewish law as well as Christ.

The Law of Christ. In chs. 5 and 6 Paul tries to convince
the Galatians that liberation from slavery under the law
means freedom to live out the law of Christ (6:2). The law
of Christ is to be free (5:1). Christian freedom is the result
of Christ's action in liberating those who believe in him,
symbolized in the church as dying and rising again
through baptism (Hans Dieter Betz). This *gift* of freedom
is at the same time a *task,* for freedom requires active

participation. In a sense we have only as much freedom as we use. The only way to stand fast in freedom is to exercise that freedom by walking and living in the Spirit (5:1, 16, 25).

Salvation is a free gift of God in Jesus Christ which needs to be lived out in our lives. It can be lost by those who think they can "help themselves" to freedom by following a prescribed set of rules rather than Christ. Verses 2–12 expand the declaration of freedom by discussing circumcision and the keeping of the law in response to the "new preachers" who claim that the Galatians must be circumcised and follow the law of the Jews in order to be saved. According to Paul, the whole law must be kept without selection or preference for what is convenient, if one decides to live under the law. In his perspective, Christ has replaced the law. The scandal of the cross is that it has liberated us from a rigidly detailed style of life (I Cor. 1:20–25). We have been accepted as righteous without the works of the law through God's grace and we are set free to become gracious neighbors.

Life in the Spirit. Freedom is "hard to handle" and is usually abandoned either to "law and order" or to unrestrained hedonism. It is this second tendency that Paul addresses in Gal. 5:13–24 by contrasting life in the Spirit and in the flesh. Here he is talking about the way an entire person (including spirit and body) either serves the Spirit of God or serves the power of sin or evil. The word "flesh" refers to the totality of fallen human existence, cut off from the redemptive love of God, not just to the body. Using a catalog of vices and virtues familiar to his readers, perhaps because they were used in preparation for baptism, Paul illustrates the chaotic fruits of life in the flesh in contrast to the unified fruits that flow from life in the Spirit. This list is not intended as a new set of rules, for there is only one limit on what is allowed in Christian freedom—belonging to Christ and sharing his life and sufferings as well as his glory (Ernst Käsemann).

Verses 25–26 move into the closing recommendations concerning living and walking by the Spirit. In Paul's thinking, Christ, the Spirit, and freedom are one:

> Now the Lord is the Spirit, and where the Spirit of the Lord is, there is freedom. (II Cor. 3:17)

Freedom in Christ is both the basis and the result of the gifts of the Spirit. Life in the Spirit is a life of freedom, an anticipation of the resurrection that is expected. Those in Christ do not need the law, for they already participate in new creation (Gal. 6:15; II Cor. 5:17). Their freedom is an anticipation of that new creation in which human existence is once again an opportunity for harmony and goodwill among all people (Gal. 6:10). By walking in this freedom, Christians "stand fast" in the one law of Christ: *Be free!*

SALVATION TODAY

In Christian tradition the word that usually describes the way we are set free in Christ and are nurtured in that freedom is "salvation." Salvation is impossible to define because it is a *story,* not an *idea* (Pauline Webb, p. 13). The story begins at the other end of history with the fulfillment of God's justice in the mending of creation and making all things new (Isa. 65:17–25; Rev. 21:1–4). God's justice or righteousness means that God has "put things right" in the world and in our lives (Krister Stendahl, p. 31). Through God's gracious action, men and women are reunited as partners with God and enabled to respond to God's love through faith. As Paul puts it in Rom. 5:1–2:

> Since we are justified by faith, we have peace with God through our Lord Jesus Christ. . . . And we rejoice in our hope of sharing the glory of God.

In accepting this story as our own we join in the story of Jesus (*Yeshua*, the one who saves). We know the end, but we nevertheless are responsible for making the whole story our own. With God's help we are set free to become helpers of others, and thus nurtured in our full humanity as partners with God.

Including the Whole Story. In 1973 the World Council of Churches gathered three hundred people in Bangkok, Thailand, to ask them the same question we struggled with in East Harlem: What is salvation today? From every context and continent people came to discuss the meaning of salvation that would speak to the cultural and spiritual background of their own nation and denomination. As the story of salvation is *situation variable*, it happens differently in the various situations where the search for meaning and hope is taking place. But the participants hoped that by sharing their diverse stories they would find a way around a particularly difficult issue in the understanding of salvation. They wanted to overcome the polarization between those Christians who had reduced the story to a doctrine of personal salvation and life after death, and other Christians who reduced the story to a program of social salvation in the lives of people who were suffering and dying.

Part of the confusion about the meaning of the story of salvation stems from the traditions of the Bible and of the early church. As we saw in the discussion of sin in Chapter 6, there was a gradual shift in the meaning due to interpretation and reinterpretation in the lives of people of faith. In the Old Testament there is no "doctrine" of salvation, but words such as "to deliver" and "to redeem" are used to describe what God has done and will do for Israel and all the nations. One of the most important words used to describe the goal of salvation is *shalom*. The word, usually translated "peace" in English, has a wide spectrum of meanings which include not only peace but also personal, familial, and social wholeness, physical well-being, and prosperity. It includes both the Exodus motif of *liberation* and deliverance from bondage and distress, and the Genesis motif of *blessing* as the power of life that creates wholeness in both creature and creation (Gen. 1:28; Claus Westermann).

In the Gospels the two motifs of liberation and blessing appear in the story of the Prince of Peace. In fulfilling the messianic promises of God's salvation, Jesus is known as Savior. He embodies the meaning of shalom through the acts of healing (blessing) as well as the action of crucifixion and resurrection (liberation). In Paul's writings such as his letter to the Galatians, and in his later epistles, the word most often used to mean salvation focuses on the divine/human relationship of justification by grace through faith. Paul speaks of salvation in three different ways: as once-and-for-all occurrence in Jesus Christ, as an ongoing process in the life of the believer, as a future realization.

In the light of the Hellenistic belief in the separation of body and soul, the early church appears to narrow the meaning of salvation further. Rather than referring to liberation and blessing of all creatures and creation, or to reconciled humanity, salvation is understood as well-being or health of the soul and its eternal destiny.

Salvation as Humanization. Many other shifts have occurred in interpreting the story of salvation, but even this brief description can help us to recognize that salvation includes and transcends the personal and the social, the physical and the spiritual, the present and the future dimensions of human existence. Just how important this is may be seen when we ask ourselves about what salvation might mean in the life of the battered woman described in Chapter 6. In the perspective of liberation and blessing, salvation might mean both freedom from the cycle of violence and financial dependence, and the possibility of physical, social, and psychological healing. In the perspec-

tive of her reconciliation to God, it might mean a transfor-
mation of her identity so that she gains an inner trust in
Christ that enables her to be free and to live out that
freedom. In the perspective of her eternal destiny it might
mean that the battered woman can find some meaning
and comfort in the assurance of a better life after death.
These meanings could *all* be important in the restoration
of this woman's full humanity. Why not include the whole
story?

One way of describing the story of salvation today in a
way that might remind us of its many dimensions would
be to say that it has to do with the total process of becoming human. Such a process of restoring broken relationships is rooted in God's act of redemption. In Christ, God
has acted to mend creation once and for all. Christ acted
as one for all in rehumanizing the world in the midst of its
dehumanization. Thus in Christ the world is set free to live
out God's purpose (Rom. 5:6–11).

God's radical help is a gift. Through God's gracious action in Christ we have been set free from sin and our
humanity restored (Rom. 5:1–5). In this sense we are *already human*. Yet, from our brief consideration of Galatians, it is clear that we not only receive this possibility of
humanity and freedom as a gift, we also have to work it out
day by day "with fear and trembling" (Phil. 2:12). By the
power of the Spirit which is at work in our lives we are in
the process of *becoming human* in the midst of our struggles with our old human nature (Rom. 7:14–15). And one
day we will be *fully human* when we are set free from the
restraint of Old Creation and fully united with God.

FREEDOM TO BE HUMAN

In Galatians, Paul reminds us that our story of new life
in Christ is a story about freedom. The one who represents
that freedom is Jesus Christ. He represents God's human-

ity and freedom in choosing to be with us. At the same time as Jesus represents our humanity and need for God's liberating help, he also represents true humanity. This true humanity shows us God's intention in creating us as helpers and partners who freely live in obedience to God's gracious will.

Horizon of Freedom. In Christ freedom has become the horizon of our lives (Hans Hoekendijk). Like any horizon, it constantly moves ahead of us as we move, beckoning us, but never captured by any one vision or action. One of the reasons for this is that freedom is universal. God wills that all might obtain "glorious liberty" (Rom. 8:21). Its universal nature means that none of us is completely free until all are free. We are joined together in a world where our freedom is always conditional on the freedom of others, and on the consequences of our actions for freedom in the lives of others.

The horizon is also moving because freedom happens in concrete situations. One person's experience of liberation may not be another's. For those struggling with the oppression of racism, the freedom related to sexism or ageism may not seem to matter as much. For the person looking for a job, the freedom not to work seems like a cruel joke. Each individual or group puts a priority on what each genuinely seeks to be free *from* and what each hopes to be free *for.* Freedom becomes good news when it is addressed to the priority needs of the people in their own context.

The horizon also moves because human freedom is not so much a fact as a possibility as women and men struggle to act and live free in their lives. For most philosophers freedom is a quality of human life itself. It is not reducible to political, economic, or even moral or psychological freedom, but has to do with human capacity for choice and for struggle against internal and external forms of bondage (Fromm and Xirau, p. 12). The qualitative aspect of freedom means that it can never be assumed that genuine actions of freedom necessarily need deprive others of their freedom. In a real sense our freedom as a quality of life *expands* as others gain freedom. Sharing freedom, like sharing love, makes it grow, not diminish, in our own lives and in society.

The moving horizon of freedom in Jesus Christ is one way of answering the basic predicament of freedom as choice. Human beings choose, yet experience their choice as determined by forces beyond their control. According to Søren Kierkegaard the paradox of human freedom is "exactly the identity of choosing and determining and of being chosen and determined" (Niebuhr, Vol. I, p. 163). In order to emphasize the gift of God's grace which sets us free to choose partnership with God and with others, many Christian theologians, such as Augustine, Luther, and Calvin, have asserted that, since the Fall, there is neither the will nor the ability to choose the freedom of Christ without God's help. In modern times philosophers such as Marx and Freud have also held that human beings were under bondage, not to sin, but to social or psychological forces from which they must be freed. The key to freedom, however, is not how much of life is determined by forces beyond our control, but whether or not there is a source of hope that keeps the possibility of freedom open. In truth it would seem that human freedom is dependent freedom. It functions fully as free will only when it is exercised in partnership with God in the way it was intended.

Freedom to Be Helped. The horizon of freedom in our lives is thus the horizon of our own humanity as we join Paul in walking in the Spirit of freedom (Gal. 5:25). In this willingness to exercise our freedom we are set free for the future, to live out our *human destiny*. That destiny is not to exercise our freedom as conquest and mastery over those who are weak, for then our freedom comes at the

expense of others (Jürgen Moltmann and M. Douglas
Meeks). The cost of freedom is justice. Without justice,
freedom belongs only to the masters. Our destiny is partnership with a God whose glory is shown in choosing to
pay the cost of freedom by becoming partner to suffering
humanity (Phil. 2:1–11). We are set free to begin living out
that future of partnership now.

The exercise of the gift of freedom also liberates us to
live out our *human nature* as freedom for others. Our
freedom does not consist of exercising our rights in compe-
tition with the rights of others. Rather, it consists of sharing in the rights of others. Created for co-humanity, we are
able to express our care for the earth and for one another
in learning to be helpers "corresponding" to one another
(Gen. 2:18). Our nature is to go beyond ourselves toward
others and toward God, finding the fulfillment of this freedom through sharing it in love (Gal. 5:25).

In our exercise of freedom we discover the possibility of
human nurture through the freedom to be helped. At last,
we are able to admit our human pride and weakness, as
well as our human selfishness and self-hate. We are able to
admit that we need the radical help of God in order to
restore our dislocated life and society. In the cross God
shared the human predicament of alienation and acted to
overcome it. Having tried every other form of security
and "self-help," we discover that what we need is God's
help. In our turning around to God, the acknowledgment
of our own weakness helps us to accept the help of God
and the help of our neighbor.

How does this freedom look to someone like my friend
from East Harlem who said salvation meant: "I'm more
free"? What did it mean in her life as a black woman,
single parent, welfare mother, with three children? Freedom for the future meant that she didn't give up! She
refused to be caught in the circle of fated poverty because
she trusted in the promise of God's partnership in her life

and that of her people. Freedom for others meant that she was being freed from helplessness and fear by acting on God's behalf as a helper of others in her own community. The problems of violence in the street, sickness in her home, poverty all around her became more "manageable" as she found strength to help others who had even greater needs. Freedom to be helped meant that she had found a Christian community that affirmed that she was worth God's help and invited her to share in God's nurturing action through the life of the church. In attending house Bible study groups, in demonstrating for better schools, in breaking open the Word and Bread of life she was finding the freedom of Christ that allowed her to *be free.*

8
BECOMING HUMAN
Luke 24:13–35

In Christ we are already free to be human. At the same time we have to walk in that freedom in order to become human (Gal. 5:1, 13, 25). Any of us who have ever been part of a freedom movement know that "keepin' on keepin' on" is not an optional feature. With its history of ministry to women around the world, the YWCA most certainly has a long track record. Yet from time to time the members of that women's movement have had to remind themselves to *keep on walking*.

Such a time for commitment came at the national convention of the YWCA in San Diego, California, in 1973. Responding to the demands of the time, the members voted resoundingly to assess their strength as a women's movement and to "chart new strategies for the elimination of racism wherever it exists and by any means necessary." The liturgy that was used to celebrate this decision was entitled "Can't Stop Now!" Together we sang: "We're on our way, and we won't turn back . . ." Together we affirmed the words of Ron Dellums that once we put our feet on the road to freedom we can't stop until "everybody on the face of the earth is walking in freedom and justice."

The exciting thing about being on our way is that it is along the difficult path toward freedom that we discover what it means to be human. Not just in our church ser-

96

vices, or at study and prayer, but all along the road of life we meet others who share our destiny and occasionally, if we keep on walking, we also meet the One who has come to help us become human.

WHAT HAPPENED ON THE ROAD

No one knows the way to Emmaus. But all the tours of the Holy Land will take you there anyway, to a place called "Emmaus" about seven miles from Jerusalem. Somehow, as you think of those other visitors along the hot, dusty road, and sit in the shade of the trees to break bread, it really doesn't matter that scholars don't know the exact location of that ancient village. Although we don't know the way to Emmaus, Christ knows the way to us. And when he joins us on the road, we give thanks!

This is what "Luke, the beloved physician," a fellow worker of Paul, would like us to discover (Col. 4:14; II Tim. 4:11; Philemon 24). He has compiled "an orderly account" of the events that occurred in the life of Jesus and his followers so that the readers can discover the presence of Christ for themselves (Luke 1:1–4). In ch. 24, Luke presents two resurrection traditions that witness to the appearance of the risen Lord in fulfillment of the Scriptures (I. Howard Marshall). In vs. 1–11, Luke opens his account with the visit of the women to the empty tomb. It is characteristic of this first-century Evangelist to include details about Jesus' women disciples even when they appear to be forgotten in other accounts (Luke 8:1–3; Joanna Dewey). The other disciples do not believe the women. They consider the women's "idle tale" mere gossip, perhaps because women were not allowed to be authoritative witnesses in Jewish tradition.

Partners Along the Way. In the resurrection accounts Luke has reached the third stage in his drama of the *Way of the Lord* (Hans Conzelmann). In the first stage God

walked with Israel as a saving, correcting, and judging
fellow traveler. In the second stage, described in the Gospel of Luke, the gracious rule of God has been manifested
in word and deed by Jesus of Nazareth and witnessed to
by his community of followers. The third stage of the Way
begins at the resurrection and ascension and is unfolded
in the book of Acts. In this stage not only eyewitnesses but
all generations, cultures, and peoples are invited to share
this incredible story.

The story of Jesus' appearance to two disciples on the
road to Emmaus is told in Luke 24: 13–27. The partners
on the road are not part of the "eleven" but are familiar
with all the resurrection events. Luke gives the name of
one of them, Cleopas, apparently because the man is well
known to the readers in Luke's church. The other traveler
could have been a woman, perhaps Cleopas' wife, or another man (I. Howard Marshall). As they report the events
of the last three days to the stranger they meet on the
road, they seem disappointed, puzzled, and much surprised that their fellow traveler does not know the news.

It appears that they are so preoccupied with their own
grief that they do not have the faith to discover Jesus as he
makes himself known in interpreting the Scriptures (vs.
27, 32, 44–49). The early church was concerned to show
that Jesus was truly the Messiah, the anointed Savior of
God's people, and, therefore, usually included references
to Christ's fulfillment of the Scriptures in its preaching. By
having Jesus interpret his own suffering, death, and glory
in the light of the Old Testament, Luke sets a precedent
for biblical interpretation and preaching by his followers.

Their Eyes Were Opened. Today we recognize that the
use of the metaphor of blindness can have a very negative
effect in reinforcing prejudice toward blind persons and
those who are physically impaired. Yet in this context the
metaphor becomes a powerful indicator, not only of God's
action but also of the way human beings are able to control

what they "see" according to their presupposition of what is going on around them (vs. 16, 31). As so often happens, they have all the *facts* but they have missed the *person*. It seems like an "impossible possibility" that the one who opened the eyes of the blind and raised the dead could himself be raised (Reinhold Niebuhr).

Verses 28–31 describe how the "stranger" finally does become known to the disciples in the breaking of bread. When Jesus accepts their invitation to supper, he is given the place of honor and invited to pronounce the blessing. The disciples discover him in this familiar action (22:19). This moment of disclosure is a moment of truth. In Greek the word "truth" means no longer hidden; a disclosure, opening up before our eyes what could not be perceived; light coming out of darkness. Truth is always *new* (Hans Hoekendijk). It has to be discovered anew by each person. When the "A-ha!" moment comes, the pieces of experience fall into place. Once Jesus reveals himself, the disciples say, "A-ha, that's what was happening on the road!" (v. 32). They are so excited that they hurry back along the road to Jerusalem to share their discovery of the risen Lord, and how he was known to them in breaking bread and opening the Scriptures along the road.

The excitement of discovery and the urge to witness is characteristic of many of the Gospel stories, such as the story of the man among the tombs and of the woman at the well, discussed in Chapters 1 and 2. It is also a frequent experience in our own lives as new things happen in unexpected ways. This is how, for instance, a Spanish evangelism program began in our church in East Harlem. It began when the janitor found himself at a Bible study session. He had never read the Bible in English and was very reluctant to join the group, but he had agreed to come to the church retreat because I needed help driving the minibus. I knew his attendance at the discussion was really in doubt when he offered to prepare lunch instead!

Even with a Spanish Bible and an illustrated Daily Bible
Reading guide he "dragged his feet." But when he saw the
pictures of the earth creature and of Adam and Eve in the
garden his eyes suddenly opened wide. This was a story he
knew well and it was one he loved to tell. After that the
only problem was that he wouldn't stop!

Eyes of Faith

What does happen when we hear God's invitation to
become newly human as followers of Christ? Surely the
process of falling in faith is as mysterious as falling in love.
Somehow a new relationship is born that gives us the vision for our freedom journey with God. *Trust in God* is
born out of the conviction that God's promise for the
mending of creation is sure. God holds our future open, so
there is always hope against hope that we may become the
human beings God intends. *Trust in ourselves* is born out
of the gift of God's acceptance. In God's choosing to be
partner with us we become subjects of our own actions
and life, rather than manipulated objects and dehumanized pawns of others. *Trust in others* is born of the knowledge that we are not only created, but called in community. Our freedom journey with others, for others, toward
God's future is made possible by helping and being helped
along the way.

Changing Consciousness. The ability to see things new
and thus to become new ourselves is related to our human
ability to transcend ourselves in relation to our world and
to other people. We are free to name and understand, or
misname and misunderstand, the reality we experience.
In doing this we express God's gift of dominion and responsibility for the world in which we dwell along with all
the other creatures of the earth.

The process of growth in understanding and changing
consciousness is familiar to us in many areas of our lives.

In our social relationships this process is often called "conscientization," a word coined in Latin America. Conscientization is learning to perceive contradictions between the way we experience social reality and the way it has been interpreted, and to take steps with others to change these contradictions (Paulo Freire). Through this process persons intentionally learn to be critical of the discrepancies between what is described by "authorities" in public life and "authorities" in private life and what actually seems to be going on. As people discover that history not only is changeable but also that it needs to be changed, they begin to act according to their new perception so that they themselves change. Thus they become more conscious of themselves as human beings capable of shaping their destiny along with others for the common good.

Such radical reorientation has been experienced, for instance, by many United States citizens as a result of the Vietnam war and the reports of U.S. support of terrorism, torture, and murder in Latin America. People move from "unquestioning patriotism" to "patriotic rage" at their own government and finally toward "new patriotism" in working with others to end U.S. aggression. Change in perception and action has been experienced by almost every marginal group in our society. Many have moved from acceptance of their marginal position to emotional rejection of social systems that turn them into the "losers" and finally toward a search for new identity and common action for change. Groups such as women, blacks, and the elderly have begun to search out the meaning of their own humanity by learning to walk in the way of freedom.

Sometimes individuals who find themselves cut off from society and dehumanized by suffering or sickness also discover this radical reorientation. One woman I heard speak in Boston told her own story of such a change of consciousness from "cancer patient" to "cancer militant." When she discovered that she had terminal cancer, she could not communicate her hurt with anyone. She blamed herself, she blamed God. And she tried to cut herself off from family and friends. Her perspective changed when she began meeting with a support group of cancer patients. In sharing her story with them she went first from inability to admit her "modern leprosy" to an ability to cope with her own life and finally to work as an advocate for others.

Conversion. In Christian tradition this process of changing consciousness and renaming reality which happens through the discovery of trust and confidence in God is called *conversion.* In the Old Testament, conversion is understood as returning to the original covenant relationship of God and the people of God. For the prophets, conversion or repentance was a total reorientation of the entire person, and a return to God in obedience and unqualified trust (Jer. 8:4; Ezek. 33:19). In the New Testament it can mean "changed mind" or "repentance." Here this process of turning around in obedience to God is initiated by Jesus Christ (Mark 1:15). Conversion is turning round in order to participate by faith in a new reality which is the future of the whole creation (Leslie Newbigin).

In the exploration of our humanity we could describe conversion as the discovery that Christ's gift of freedom to be human is the answer to our search for humanity. We saw in Chapter 6 that sin is the refusal to be radically helped by God, the desire to "help ourselves" and to build our own security and guarantees. Turning away from that human sinfulness toward God is an acceptance of the radical help needed for us to live by trust in the promise of God. In conversion we discover the radical help we need, and this causes a *radical shift in perspective.* We no longer see things from the old human point of view but from the point of view of God (II Cor. 5:16–17).

This in turn causes a *radical shift in our lives* and helps our perspective and lives to continue changing and growing. Gradually we learn to walk in the way of freedom, able to help and to be helped as human beings. As our response to God's gracious initiative of partnership in our lives, conversion is a process that continues to happen our whole lives, requiring a continued willingness to walk worthy of the call of Christ.

The experience of becoming human occurs in many small ways along the journey of our lives. Such a fragmentary experience happened to me not long ago when I lost the sight of one eye in a freak accident. Out of that experience I discovered a different perspective on reality. Small things didn't matter as much to me in the light of major issues of sight and health, and partnership with caring people. Yet, at the same time as I was growing in courage, my perception of the reality of pain in the world and in my life was heightened so that my vulnerability and dependence on God were increased. This discovery that I was becoming at one and the same time both *stronger* and *weaker* was a small sign that God was patiently helping me to become more human.

NEW EXODUS

In Galatians 5, Paul exhorts us to be free and to stand firm by walking in the Spirit of freedom. He seems to be talking "nonsense," as in that slogan: "Don't do something. Stand there!" But it is not nonsense, for he is describing human nature as essentially "a way of life." Over and over in his letters Paul points out that one *walks* or lives according to the basic commitment of one's life to a particular *way* (Hans Dieter Betz). Standing in Christ's freedom means that freedom is one's way of life. To be free is to join God's freedom movement.

Walking Worthy. The exercise of this freedom is usually described as "walking worthy of God" (I Thess. 2:12; 4:1).

To be worthy is to act in a way that gives honor to God in response to God's gracious action (Phil. 2:1–11). Just as Israel understood obedience to God as "walking in the law," Paul understood the Christian way of life as "walking in Christ." Instruction in this way of life happened as Christians walked in the Way of the Lord (Acts 19:9, 23; 24:14). Christians were nurtured in Christ and became new human beings by participating in the life of the people of the Way (Eph. 4:11–16).

In this understanding of human life, persons learn to be Christian by sharing in the Christian story with others. They learn, not by memorizing the lists of vices and virtues, but by discovering what the presence of Christ means in the lives of those around them. This makes human nurture very difficult, for it happens in community as people discover the meaning of their humanity as a lived reality. Such communities are not always so easy to find, and they are certainly not so easy to live with, because the gospel message disturbs the comfortable. Fortunately, the most important gift of the Spirit is not perfection but *faithfulness,* a willingness to walk in the love of God. In the words of the songwriter Doris Ellzey Blesoff:

> We're travelin' on a road we've never seen
> before and O it's hard to know which way to go.
> (Pp. 2–3)

But as the Spirit "keeps breaking in our lives" we find the courage to live out of trust in God's promise.

Growth in our humanity takes place as *we learn to be helpers by being helped.* God has created us to be helpers of one another, and the way we discover the joy of helping is by helping others and being helped. We know that it is the relationship of love and care in families that helps children grow up as loving and caring persons. Yet we often forget this in our churches, finding it easier to expect people to become human by learning "sound doctrine."

Instruction in the faith is important, but it is only a pointer to explain why it is that we walk as we do.

God's Freedom Movement. In the Hebrew/Christian tradition, exodus has been the name of our journey. Whether we point to freedom experienced in the exodus from bondage to Pharaoh, or in the New Exodus from bondage to sin and death, we understand this freedom to be a gift of the God who redeems us from personal and societal bondage, reclaiming us as partners in New Creation. Our nurture in new humanity can also be seen as part of that journey toward freedom and wholeness. From this perspective we could even describe *education as exodus,* going out together as part of God's freedom movement. This freedom movement is God's promised action in history to set all of creation free from bondage to human decay and to establish the kingdom *on earth.* It is a movement long overdue, for, in the words of Paul:

> The created universe is waiting on tiptoe for the children of God to show what they are. (Rom. 8:19; tr. by Hans Hoekendijk)

It is the good news of the Emmaus story that freedom is already on its way. It emerges over the horizon as the firstfruits of God's New Creation are experienced in the presence of "the Spirit that keeps breaking in our lives" (Doris Ellzey Blesoff). In Luke's story the disciples are not so sure that freedom is on its way. Their expectation was that the coming of the Messiah would bring the establishment of the kingdom of God and the final resurrection. The surprise of the resurrection for them was not that one person was raised, but that everyone was not raised (Ernst Käsemann). Luke tells the story to vindicate Jesus' Messiahship and point toward a general resurrection (Acts 4:2; 17:18). At the same time, however, he shows that the freedom movement has begun in the continuing presence of Christ with the disciples along the way.

Those who have discovered that presence in their lives may not be able to define what it means to *be human,* but they are already in the process of *becoming human.* For human nurture happens by God's reconciling grace as we join in God's New Exodus. Christ has set us free. We have only to *join God's freedom movement* and to *keep walking!*

QUESTIONS FOR STUDY AND REFLECTION

SUGGESTIONS FOR GROUP STUDY
OF THE BIBLICAL TEXTS

1. Read aloud the Bible passage for a chapter and share together the *questions* you would like to raise concerning the text or the theme of the chapter.

2. Discuss the questions in the light of the original *context* of the passage, as well as in the light of what the text means for persons in a similar circumstance today.

3. Share *stories* and descriptions of actions that illuminate the text in your own life and in the life of persons you know or have read about.

4. Discuss possible *clues* from the text about God's intention for our life and world.

Chapter 1. SEARCHING FOR HUMANITY

1. What are the key words you would use to describe your own sense of self-identity?

2. What or who are the sources of authority in your life?

3. What do you think are the most important ingredients of being human?

Chapter 2. NOT QUITE HUMAN

1. Describe the characteristics of women and men as they are portrayed in television advertising.

2. Why is it that the gospel is good news for the poor and for the losers of society?

3. How would you describe the hierarchy of relationships in the informal and formal structures of your church?

Chapter 3. HUMAN DESTINY

1. What is God's intention for our lives? If the intention is for partnership, what implications does this have for our actions?

2. In what sense would you say that God is a humanist? Would you be willing to call yourself a humanist?

3. What are the most important images of the future in your own life?

Chapter 4. MORE THAN HUMAN

1. In what sense can you understand Jesus Christ as both more than human and less than human?

2. What are the sources of power in our lives? What are the sources of power among nations?

3. What experiences have you had of the discovery of power and glory in the midst of suffering?

Chapter 5. HUMAN NATURE

1. In what ways do you consider man and woman to be the same, and in what ways are they different?

2. What do you think it means to say that we are created, male and female, in the image of God?

3. In what settings would you think of yourself as "helper"? Is this a term of empowerment for you?

Chapter 6. LESS THAN HUMAN

1. In what circumstance is it most difficult for you to be helped by others?

2. In what ways do you recognize the story of the Fall taking place in your own life and community?

3. In asking the human race to exercise dominion, what responsibility does God give us for the earth and for our neighbors?

Chapter 7. HUMAN NURTURE

1. What are your favorite words, stories, or hymns that illustrate the way God's free gift of salvation happens in our lives?

2. Why is it that the gifts of the Spirit often lead persons to a more narrow and restricted life, rather than to walking in freedom?

3. Discuss the ways in which human beings have freedom of choice and the ways in which they are not free to choose.

Chapter 8. BECOMING HUMAN

1. What are some of the most important stages in your own life process of becoming human?

2. In what ways does Christ help you to see things differently, to have a different perspective on life than some of your neighbors have?

3. How can the Christian community model its formal and informal educational experiences so that they nurture persons in becoming human?

BOOKS FOR FURTHER READING

Chapter 1. SEARCHING FOR HUMANITY

LeFevre, Perry. *Understandings of Man.* Westminster Press, 1966.

Moltmann, Jürgen. *Man: Christian Anthropology in the Conflicts of the Present,* tr. by John Sturdy. Fortress Press, 1974.

Rilke, Rainer Maria. *Letters to a Young Poet,* rev. ed., tr. by M. D. H. Norton. W. W. Norton & Co., 1954.

Russell, Letty M. *Human Liberation in a Feminist Perspective—A Theology.* Westminster Press, 1974.

Chapter 2. NOT QUITE HUMAN

Birch, Bruce C., and Rasmussen, Larry L. *The Predicament of the Prosperous.* Westminster Press, 1978.

Crossan, John Dominic. *The Dark Interval: Towards a Theology of Story.* Argus Communications, 1975.

Gray, Elizabeth Dodson. *Green Paradise Lost.* 2d ed. Roundtable Press, 1979.

Nacpil, Emerito P., and Elwood, Douglas J. *The Human and the Holy: Asian Perspectives on Christian Theology.* Orbis Books, 1980.

Sayers, Dorothy L. *Are Women Human?* Wm. B. Eerdmans Publishing Co., 1947.

Wahlberg, Rachel Conrad. *Jesus According to a Woman.* Paulist/Newman Press, 1975.

Chapter 3. HUMAN DESTINY

Barth, Karl. *The Faith of the Church: A Commentary on the Apostles' Creed According to Calvin's Catechism,* ed. by Jean-Louis Leuba, tr. by Gabriel Vahanian. Meridian Books, 1958.

————. *The Humanity of God.* John Knox Press, 1960.

Nelson, Jack A. *Hunger for Justice: The Politics of Food and Faith.* Orbis Books, 1980.

Peters, Ted. *Fear, Faith, and the Future: Affirming Christian Hope in the Face of Doomsday Prophecies.* Augsburg Publishing House, 1980.

Russell, Letty M. *The Future of Partnership.* Westminster Press, 1974.

Chapter 4. MORE THAN HUMAN

Han, Wan Sang, "Meditation," in *Varieties of Witnesses,* ed. by D. Preman Niles and T. K. Thomas. Christian Conference of Asia, 480 Lorong 2, Toa Payoh, Singapore 1231, 1980.

Hoekendijk, Hans. *Horizons of Hope.* Tidings Press, 1970.

Soelle, Dorothee, "When He Came," *Revolutionary Patience* [poems], tr. by Rita and Robert Kimber. Orbis Books, 1977.

————. *Suffering,* tr. by Everett R. Kalin. Fortress Press, 1975.

Chapter 5. HUMAN NATURE

Barth, Karl. *Church Dogmatics: A Selection,* ed. by G. W. Bromiley. Harper Torchbooks, 1962.

Bird, Phyllis, "Images of Women in the Old Testament,"

in *Religion and Sexism*, ed. by Rosemary Radford Ruether. Simon & Schuster, 1974.

Jewett, Paul K. *Man as Male and Female*. Wm. B. Eerdmans Publishing Co., 1975.

Trible, Phyllis. *God and the Rhetoric of Sexuality*, ed. by W. Brueggemann and J. Donahue. Fortress Press, 1978.

Watkins, Keith. *Faithful and Fair: Transcending Sexist Language in Worship*. Abingdon Press, 1981.

Chapter 6. LESS THAN HUMAN

Eagleson, John, and Scharper, Philip, comps. *The Radical Bible*, adapted from *Bibel Provokativ*, ed. by Hellmut Haug and Jürgen Rump, tr. by Erika J. Rapp.

Fackre, Gabriel. *The Christian Story: A Narrative Interpretation of Basic Christian Doctrine*. Wm. B. Eerdmans Publishing Co., 1978.

Niebuhr, Reinhold. *The Nature and Destiny of Man*, Vols. I and II. Charles Scribner's Sons, 1941.

Saiving, Valerie, "The Human Situation: A Feminine View," in *Womanspirit Rising: A Feminist Reader in Religion*, ed. by Carol Christ and Judith Plaskow. Harper & Row, 1979.

Westermann, Claus. *Creation*, tr. by John J. Scullion. Fortress Press, 1974.

Chapter 7. HUMAN NURTURE

Cone, James H. *God of the Oppressed*. Seabury Press, 1975.

Fromm, Erich, and Xirau, Ramón, eds. *The Nature of Man: Readings*. Macmillan Co., 1968.

Käsemann, Ernst. *Jesus Means Freedom*. Fortress Press, 1978.

Stendahl, Krister. *Paul Among Jews and Gentiles.* Fortress Press, 1976.
Webb, Pauline. *Salvation Today.* SCM Press, 1974.

Chapter 8. BECOMING HUMAN

Blesoff, Doris Ellzey, "We Are Gathered," in *Everflowing Streams: Songs for Worship,* ed. by Ruth Duck and Michael G. Bausch. Pilgrim Press, 1981.
Gonzalez, Justo L., and Gonzalez, Catherine Gunsalus. *Liberation Preaching: The Pulpit and the Oppressed.* Abingdon Press, 1980.
Miller, Jean Baker. *Toward a New Psychology of Women.* Beacon Press, 1977.
Russell, Letty M. *Growth in Partnership.* Westminster Press, 1981.
Segundo, Juan Luis. *Grace and the Human Condition,* tr. by John Drury. Orbis Books, 1973.